the
real greek
at home

the
real greek
at home

DISHES FROM THE HEART
OF THE GREEK KITCHEN

THEODORE KYRIAKOU
AND CHARLES CAMPION

photographs by JASON LOWE

MITCHELL BEAZLEY

The Real Greek at Home
by Theodore Kyriakou and Charles Campion

An Hachette Livre UK Company

First published in Great Britain in 2004 by Mitchell Beazley,
an imprint of Octopus Publishing Group Limited, 2–4 Heron Quays, London E14 4JP.
www.octopusbooks.co.uk

First published in paperback in 2008

ISBN 978 1 84533 4512
A CIP catalogue record for this book is available from the British Library.

While all reasonable care has been taken during the preparation of this edition, neither the publisher, editors, nor the authors can accept responsibility for any consequences arising from the use thereof or from the information contained therein.

Commissioning Editor: Rebecca Spry
Executive Art Editor: Yasia Williams
Design: Miranda Harvey
Photography: Jason Lowe
Editor: Susan Fleming
Recipe Tester: Jane Suthering
Proofreader: Siobhán O'Connor
Production: Sarah Rogers
Index: John Noble

Typeset in Formata and Simoncini Garamond
Printed and bound by
Toppan Printing Company, China

Greece in Britain is a nationwide series of events, presented by the Hellenic Foundation for Culture, UK to illustrate the wealth and diversity of contemporary Greek culture.
www.GreeceInBritain.org.uk
http://www.GreeceInBritain.org.uk

contents

introduction

A couple of years after the publication of *Real Greek Food*
I started to get restless. Like music, cooking is more art than
science, and as with music new influences and experiences
interact with even the most traditional recipes to change them
subtly. In this book I return to the fabulous store of recipes
that were a part of my childhood and homeland, recipes that
sum up Greece and what it means to be Greek. It is my belief
that recipes can be the most wonderful shorthand for a sense
of place; they can express the kind of philosophy that is so
deeply ingrained it becomes more like an instinct; and they can
speak for the accumulated wisdom of generations. No sooner
had I made the decision to start work than images started to
come flooding back. I stopped dreaming about my old parental
home and started living the flavours and textures of these
dishes – dishes that come from the heart of a Greek kitchen.
Theodore Kyriakou, London, December 2003

festival food

For Greeks, food is such an integral part of life and culture that a glance at the dishes on the table can be as good as looking at the calendar. All the big festivals have their special dishes – for instance, the rich pork with figs that is often served at Christmas; or beef cooked with the noodle-like *hilopites*, a dish that symbolizes rebirth and regeneration; or *pastitsada*, an awesomely rich, slow-cooked stew that makes any grand occasion even more special.

braised beef with hilopites and avgolemono

μοσχάρι με χυλοπίτες αυγοκομμένες

My father is convinced that when Marco Polo took the idea of pasta from the Chinese and brought it back to Italy, he was only following in the footsteps of the brave Greek who filched the recipe for hilopites *– a kind of superior Greek ribbon pasta – from the East in a similar fashion. As kids we had to listen to endless tales muddling the exploits of Marco Polo and* hilopites. *You will always find* hilopites *in my parents' larder, as it is the perfect stand-by.*

serves 8

1 x 3kg (6½lb) piece of beef
   shin, bone in, most of the fat
   trimmed off
4 garlic cloves, quartered
100ml (3½fl oz) olive oil
100ml (3½fl oz) red wine
1kg (2¼lb) leeks, trimmed and
   finely chopped
1 litre (1¾ pints) veal stock
   plus 1 litre (1¾ pints) water
   (or all water)
salt and pepper to taste
500g (18oz) small carrots
500g (18oz) *hilopites* (or egg
   tagliatelle)
1 bunch flat-leaf parsley, finely
   chopped

avgolemono sauce

4 eggs, separated
juice of 2 large or 3 small lemons

1   Make incisions in the meat and insert the garlic quarters. Heat the olive oil in a large saucepan and brown the meat on all sides over a very low heat, with the lid on. Add the red wine to deglaze the pan, then add the leeks.

2   Heat the stock and water together in a second saucepan and bring to a simmer. Adjust the seasoning, pour over the meat and leeks, cover and simmer over a low to medium heat for about 2 hours. You will need to skim the surface from time to time.

3   Add the carrots and cook until the meat is very tender and almost falling off the bone, which will take about 45 minutes more. Keep skimming the surface as the meat cooks.

4   Add the *hilopites* and simmer for about 7 minutes. Should the noodles get too dry, you can always add a little warm water. Do not drain, but set the pot aside. At this point the *hilopites* should be barely tender.

5   To make the sauce, whisk the egg whites to soft peaks in a mixing bowl. Add a ladleful of the broth from the pan a little at a time. Fold into the whites with the lemon juice, and finally fold in the egg yolks.

6   Pour the sauce in the pan with the meat and *hilopites*, add the parsley and stir. Leave in a warm place for 5–10 minutes: the eggs will thicken the juices as the *hilopites* finish cooking. Season if necessary.

7   Cut up the meat and serve with the *hilopites*, and with the leeks and carrots if you wish.

pastitsada

πασΤιΤσάδα

Pastitsada must be eaten without a timetable. You cannot rush this kind of food, and it makes its own kind of special occasion. In our household no one was allowed to leave the table until the pot was clean and the red wine had run out. When I prepare this in the restaurant I occasionally get flashbacks to the endless political arguments that used to roll around the table. They were usually started by my father but seldom finished!

serves 4

1 x 2kg (4½lb) shin of veal
salt and pepper to taste
8 garlic cloves, coarsely chopped
juice and finely grated zest of
  1 orange
200ml (7fl oz) olive oil
75ml (2½fl oz) aged Corinthian
  red wine vinegar
1kg (2¼lb) shallots, peeled
500ml (18fl oz) veal stock
  (bought or home-made, or even
  chicken stock)
½ tsp sweet paprika
500g (18oz) dried pasta
  (macaroni or penne)
150g (5½oz) dry Mizithra cheese
  (a dry and hard sheep's milk
  whey cheese) or Kefalotiri
  cheese (a hard sheep's milk
  cheese), or pecorino, grated
1 bunch coriander, finely chopped

1 Ask your butcher to bone out the shin of veal, unless you feel confident enough to do the job yourself.

2 Lay the meat out, season it lightly, then spread over the garlic and orange zest. Roll it up and tie with butcher's string.

3 Pour half the olive oil into a large pan, heat it through, then use it to seal the roll of meat on all sides. At the end of the sealing the veal will stick to the bottom of the pan. Use the red wine vinegar to deglaze the pan and scrape up all the crispy bits.

4 Add the shallots and the stock and let it come to simmering point. Skim the surface. Add the orange juice and paprika, and adjust the seasoning with salt and pepper. Do not fully season at this point as the veal will remain on the stove for a long while and flavours tend to concentrate. Let it simmer with the lid on for 1½ hours.

5 Stir the pasta into the pan and cook for just 5 minutes, as you need the pasta to be only half cooked. Remove the pan from the heat, add the cheese, and let everything rest for 20 minutes while the pasta continues to soak up the juices. Sprinkle on the coriander and stir well.

6 Remove the shin, slice it and serve it with the pasta, which should be perfectly cooked. Drizzle the remaining olive oil over each serving.

christmas pork with figs

χριστουγεννιάτικο χοιρινό με σύκα κύμης

During the last week before the start of the academic year, my father would take the family on a trip to Kymi in Evia to buy fresh figs. When we got home, the next chore was to arrange the figs on the rooftop of our house to dry in the sun, so that by Christmas they would be at their best. This dish marries the sweetness of poached figs with tender pork.

serves 6

500g (18oz) chickpeas, soaked overnight, rinsed and drained
4 bay leaves
1 x 5-chop loin of pork, boned by the butcher and skinned, but with the fat left on
coarse sea salt and black pepper
1 tbsp each ground cumin, nutmeg and cinnamon
250g (9oz) poached figs (see page 56)
1kg (2¼lb) button onions, peeled
1kg (2¼lb) small potatoes, peeled and quartered
1 x 400g jar tomato *perasti* (the Greek equivalent of tomato passata)
125ml (4fl oz) olive oil
thick Greek yoghurt, to serve

1 Bring the chickpeas to a boil in a large pan with fresh water and the bay leaves, skimming the foam off the surface from time to time. Boil for 10 minutes, then simmer over a low heat for 30–40 minutes, until slightly softened. Drain thoroughly.

2 Preheat the oven to 220°C/425°F/gas mark 7.

3 While the chickpeas are cooking, score the pork fat and rub it well with coarse sea salt. Rub all the spices into the meat.

4 Make a cut in the eye of the meat lengthways – you are aiming to create a pocket. Open the meat out and arrange the poached figs along its length. Fold the flap back and roll up the joint, tying it with butcher's string. Reserve the syrup from the figs.

5 Place the pork in a large roasting tray and add the drained chickpeas, button onions, potato, tomato *perasti* and olive oil. Stir, and pour in additional water if necessary to keep everything but the pork covered.

6 Roast the pork for 20 minutes, then turn down the temperature to 180°C/350°F/gas mark 4. Cook for a further 1½ hours, or until the meat and chickpeas are very tender. Add boiling water as necessary if the vegetable mix looks like drying out. Adjust the seasoning with salt and pepper.

7 When it comes out of the oven, rub the pork with the reserved syrup from the figs. Let the meat rest for at least 20 minutes before you carve. Serve with the chickpeas and a bowl of thick Greek yoghurt.

kiskekis

ΚΕΣΚΕΚΙ

So much Greek food is based on flour: breads, pasta and pies. We are probably the only nation in the world that is happy to eat pasta and bread together. One of my favourite regional pastas is kiskekis, *and it always reminds me of the old-fashioned type of delicatessen my father used to run in the old part of Athens. This is an egg and milk pasta usually made with semolina, but occasionally with bulgur or wheat flour, then rubbed through a fine sieve so it ends up as small grains.*

serves 4

200g (7oz) *kiskekis* (or couscous)
juice of 6 oranges and finely
    grated zest of 3 oranges
juice and finely grated zest of
    2 lemons
1 bunch flat-leaf parsley, chopped
salt and pepper to taste
2 chilli peppers (or more to taste)
1 x 2kg (4½lb) pork shoulder
    joint, on the bone but rind
    removed
50ml (2fl oz) olive oil
100ml (3½fl oz) white wine
1 litre (1¾ pints) chicken stock
250g (9oz) shallots, quartered
4 bay leaves
1 tsp ground cumin
strained Greek yoghurt, to serve

1 Put the *kiskekis* in a bowl with the orange and lemon juice and zest. Add the parsley and season with salt and pepper. Leave to infuse, preferably somewhere warm.

2 Burn the chillies over a flame. When the skin turns black, scrape it off, cut the chillies in half, and discard the seeds.

3 With the handle of a wooden spoon, drive two holes through the length of the pork and stuff it with the chillies and some seasoning.

4 Heat the olive oil in a large heavy-bottomed casserole and brown off the meat over a low heat. You shouldn't blacken the pork fat, as you need it to melt slowly during the cooking process. Add the wine and scrape up the bits from the bottom of the casserole. Turn the temperature down as low as possible and cook for an hour with the lid on.

5 Warm the stock. Pour it over the meat, then add the shallots, bay leaves, cumin, and seasoning. Cover, and let it simmer for 1½–2 hours, or until very tender. Turn off the heat and let the meat rest in the pan for 30 minutes. By now all the citrus juices should have been absorbed.

6 Arrange the *kiskekis* on a platter and pour over some of the cooking juices from the meat – you are aiming for a soupy texture. Slice the pork, which should be falling off the bone. Spare cooking juices are worth saving as they make for a good, meaty stock. Serve the *kiskekis* with the pork and strained yoghurt.

ginger beer with
saint spiridon

In Kerkyra (the Greek name for both Corfu Town and the island itself), the Easter celebrations are quite different to those elsewhere in Greece. There is a huge festival which brings together a wide range of faiths and beliefs – Orthodox Christians, the Roman Catholic community, Venetian influences, heathen traditions, and, at the core of everything, Spiridon, the island's own saint – with a general feel-good factor created by the bright spring weather. If you were to hurry, the journey from our house in Halandri to Kerkyra would take six or seven hours, but my father liked to take his time, admire the countryside, and stop off intermittently – on the one occasion the whole family went to Kerkyra for Easter it took us no less than three days to get there! My father had planned the trip in such a way so as to arrive in Kerkyra on Palm Sunday. That is the day when the body of Saint Spiridon is paraded around the streets followed by all the town's orchestras. During the plague of 1630, Kerkyra was saved due to the intervention of Saint Spiridon, and each year the procession sets off from the saint's church in the morning and follows the line of the old town walls, from where Saint Spiridon drove off the plague. By lunchtime the whole island is sitting down to a meal of salt cod.

In the build-up to the big day – Greeks celebrate the Resurrection – my father led us out of the town and out into the villages. He wanted us to see the elegant Venetian houses and the *tavernas* that had set their tables out in the sun. He wanted us to try the tasty Lenten dishes and the local wine, which was at its best. As soon as the sun had set we would head for the local *kafenein* and try Greek coffee and sweet liqueurs.

Then, as now, the most striking feature of Easter in Kerkyra was the moving church music that spilled out of the places of worship and filled the alleyways. This choral chanting, a form of four-voice harmony, came from Crete during the 17th century, and is known as "Cretan music". And then there are the orchestras, for Good Friday is the day of the Epitaphios, the funeral of Christ. So the Old Philharmonic Orchestra in red uniform plays Albinoni's *Adagio*, the Mantzaros Orchestra in blue Verdi's *Marcia Funebre*, and the Kapodistrias Orchestra the *Elegia Funebre*, Mariana's *Sventura,* and Chopin's *Funeral March.*

On Holy Saturday the people of Kerkyra have their own version of an old Venetian New Year custom – they throw clay jars from the balconies and windows in the old town. The Venetians believed that the New Year would bring them new replacements, but for the Greeks it is simply an expression of the exuberance of Easter and the joys of spring. The Lenten fast is broken and the Resurrection celebrated with *magiritsa* (Easter soup), red eggs, and *columbines* (a special bread of Venetian origin, baked in the form of a dove).

But my father would not stick strictly to the traditional tourist delights and made a point of seeking out regional specialities such as *tsitsibira* (ginger beer). This used to be famous on all seven Ionian Islands and is a legacy from the time of the British, but now it is only made in Corfu. Using lemon juice, natural lemon oil, grated ginger, water, and sugar, one small factory on the island brews this soft drink in huge cauldrons. It is served in local cafés between Easter and autumn.

My family is obsessed with food, and Kerkyra has the right food for the right season. There's *sofritto* (beef stewed in a white sauce with white pepper and garlic, a dish of Franco-Venetian origin) on Sundays, *pastitsada* at celebrations, and *horta* (boiled greens) for everyday meals. In winter there's *bourdetto* (made with firm fish, usually scorpion fish, cooked in a sauce containing plenty of red pepper) or beans and *renga* (kippered herrings), and on 25 March, to celebrate both the Annunciation and Independence Day, there is salt cod and *skordalia* (garlic sauce).

On Easter Tuesday at five in the afternoon, at the Church of Saint Spiridon, the saint is returned to his casket, in a ceremony known as the *"basmata"*. Our Easter holiday had finished.

chicken sofritto

κοτόπουλο σοφρίτο

On the island of Kerkyra the local dialect has thousands of words and phrases that have been 'borrowed' from Italian. One such is "sofritto", the name of a simple dish that has become a speciality at local festivals. Originally, it was made with fillets of veal that were first fried and then cooked slowly, like in a stew, with garlic, black pepper, and parsley. When on holidays with my parents, this was one of our favourite summery supper dishes. A cold salad of courgettes was always on the table, and the lemony jelly from the chicken was good enough to squabble over.

serves 4

1 x 1.5–2kg (3½–4½lb) "happy"
  chicken
100ml (3½fl oz) olive oil
juice and finely grated zest of
  1 lemon
1 cinnamon stick
1 bunch flat-leaf parsley, washed
  and left whole
2 bay leaves
2 garlic cloves
200ml (7fl oz) water
salt and pepper to taste

1   Put the chicken in a heavy-bottomed casserole and surround it with the other ingredients. Season to taste, then bring to the boil, lower the heat, place the lid on, and simmer until the chicken is very tender and cooked through – about 60–70 minutes. Turn the chicken over a couple of times during cooking. If you see that the chicken needs longer and that all the liquid has evaporated, refresh with some more hot water. When the chicken is cooked, remove the pan from the heat, check the seasoning of the broth, and let it cool.

2   Bone the chicken and arrange the pieces in a deep bowl. Pour the sauce over, cover, and place the bowl in the refrigerator. A few hours later, the liquid should have set and become a pale, lemony jelly. Serve cold.

button onions with saffron

κρεμμυδάκια στιφάδου με ζαφορά

These saffron onions come to the table for special Friday meals. They are particularly good with pan-fried fish or scallops, but they are also good with any cold meat that you have left over from lunch.

serves 4

40g (1½oz) butter

50ml (2fl oz) olive oil

125g (4½oz) thyme honey

2 cloves

½ nutmeg, freshly grated

350ml (12fl oz) white wine

1kg (2¼lb) button or pickling
  onions, peeled

1 pinch saffron strands, crushed in
  an eggcup of boiling water

salt and pepper to taste

1   Put the butter, olive oil, honey, spices, and wine into a saucepan and bring to the boil. Add the button onions and simmer for 30 minutes. Keep de-frothing while simmering. Add the saffron and a pinch of salt and pepper and simmer until the onions are cooked but still retain some crunch – about another 5–10 minutes. Strain the onions into a jar.

2   Return the cooking juices to the stove and boil to reduce by almost half. Pour this reduced liquid over the onions.

3   These will keep well in the refrigerator for at least 1 month. Let them reach room temperature before serving.

"As soon as the sun had set we would head for the local kafenein *and try Greek coffee and sweet liqueurs. Then, as now, the most striking feature of Easter in Kerkyra was the moving church music that spilled out of the places of worship and filled the alleyways."*

chocolate truffles

τρούφες σοκολάτας

These almond and orange truffles are sold by weight and come in the most beautiful packaging. They are a treat reserved for high days and holidays.

makes about 25 truffles

125g (4½oz) orange peel, pith removed, from about 10 large organic or unwaxed oranges

125g (4½oz) shelled whole almonds

125g (4½oz) white sugar

25g (1oz) unsalted butter

100g (3½oz) dark chocolate (at least 65% cocoa solids)

25g (1oz) cocoa powder

1   Preheat the oven to 180°C/350°F/gas mark 4.

2   Blanch the orange peel in boiling water until soft – this will take around 3 minutes. Drain and chop coarsely.

3   Blanch the almonds in boiling water and rub off the skins. Chop the nuts fairly finely and roast on a baking tray until they just turn golden – about 15 minutes.

4   Put the almonds, sugar, and orange peel in a large saucepan over a low heat. Stir with a wooden spoon until the sugar melts. The mixture is ready when it does not stick to the inside of the pan and leaves it clean as you stir.

5   Let the mixture cool down until it is malleable, then work in the butter and roll it into small balls on a cold surface.

6   Melt the chocolate in a bowl set over a pan of just simmering water and put the cocoa powder on a plate. Dip the nutty balls in the chocolate and finally roll them in the cocoa powder. Leave to set hard in the refrigerator.

dishes from the mountains

Wild food such as rabbit; simple ingredients such as eggs, aromatic herbs, and strong cheeses; pickled and preserved foods – these are the threads that run through Greek mountain cooking. Dishes are strongly flavoured, often hearty, and have an integrity that stems from the mountain people who created them. It is simple cookin, but with intense flavours; dishes such as rabbit with almonds, eggs with nettles, pork with black-eye beans, and bread made with yoghurt.

rabbit mountain style

κουνέλι του βουνού

This rabbit dish guarantees plenty of finger licking and will herald the low murmur of voices and a good many empty bottles as cold beer does battle with a ready thirst.

serves 4

1 rabbit, skinned and cleaned
juice and finely grated zest of
  2 lemons
1 bunch mountain thyme
  or lemon thyme
100ml (3½fl oz) olive oil
salt and pepper to taste

1   Joint the rabbit: you should end up with two hind legs, two pieces each with a shoulder and front leg, and the saddle. Cut the saddle across into three or four even pieces.

2   Place the rabbit pieces in a mixing bowl with the lemon juice, zest, thyme, and olive oil. Cover the bowl with clingfilm and marinate at room temperature for an hour. Turn the pieces in the marinade a few times.

3   Preheat a heavy-bottomed skillet for a few minutes – you want it hot. This dish also works well cooked over an open wood or charcoal fire.

4   Reduce the heat under the pan (or lift it away), season the rabbit pieces, then cook until nicely browned and cooked all the way through – about 10–15 minutes. If you are cooking over wood or charcoal, wait until the coals glow red and are covered with ash before starting. Keep brushing the rabbit pieces with marinade as they cook.

5   When the rabbit is ready, serve hot. It must be eaten with the fingers.

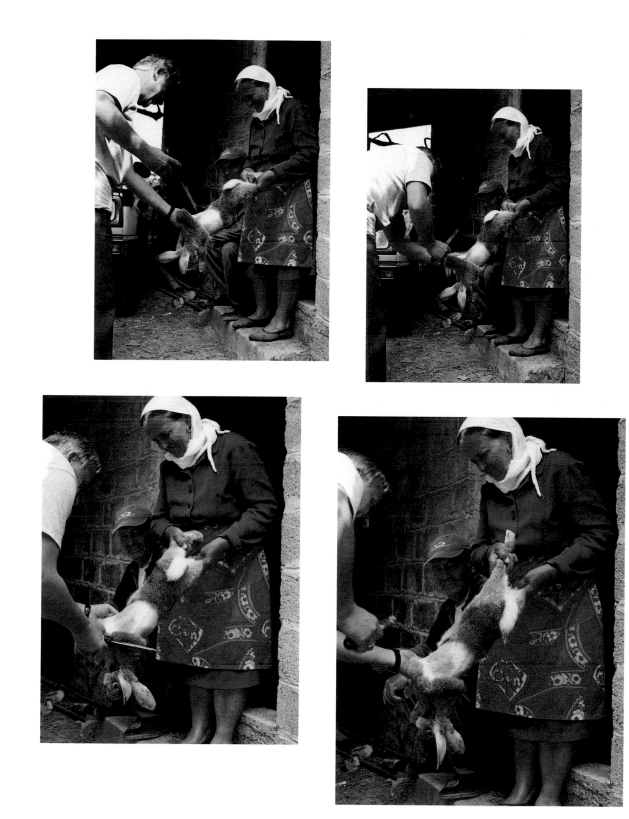

rabbit with fresh almonds

κουνέλι με φρέσκα αμύγδαλα

Sometimes I get the chance of a flying visit home in early spring, and for a couple of days before I go I worry in case the arrangements fall through. During these periods the pressure is on and I smoke and drink more than I ought, yet every morning I wake up fresh as a daisy. The smell of this rabbit dish from the mountains wafting out of my mother's kitchen is the only certain hangover cure I know. The best almonds for the dish are sold by Mediterranean shops in early spring, when the shells are still soft. If you can get them, remember that they keep well in the freezer.

serves 4

1 whole rabbit, skinned and
   cleaned
juice of 1 lemon
salt and pepper to taste
225ml (8fl oz) olive oil
150g (5½oz) shallots, finely diced
750g (1lb 10oz) tomatoes, skinned,
   seeded, and finely chopped
500g (18oz) fresh "green" almonds
   in shell, shelled (blanched
   almonds are a poor second best:
   use only 250g/9oz)
1 bunch thyme, leaves only
55g (2oz) cold butter
100g (3½oz) plain flour
125ml (4fl oz) white wine
200ml (7fl oz) chicken stock

1 Cut the legs off the rabbit and cut the back into three to four pieces. Keep all the trimmings, carcass, and offal in a bowl. Wash the rabbit portions with the lemon juice and season with salt.

2 In a heavy-bottomed pan, heat 100ml (3½fl oz) of the olive oil and sauté the shallots. When soft, add the tomato and almonds, and simmer until the sauce starts to thicken – about 20–30 minutes. Remove from the heat, add the thyme, adjust the seasoning, and set aside, covered.

3 In another heavy-bottomed frying pan, melt the butter with 50ml (2fl oz) of the olive oil. Flour the rabbit portions and pan-fry them until they are cooked through – stay close to the stove and turn the pieces as they colour. Your oil should never be very hot. The pieces of back will be ready first, then the front legs. As they are cooked, remove them from the pan and put them into the tomato and almond sauce.

4 Discard 80 per cent of the oil. Flour all the reserved trimmings and offal, and pan-fry them. Keep frying and turning for 5 minutes, then add the white wine. Increase the heat and let most of the wine evaporate. Pour in the chicken stock and reduce by 75 per cent. Push through a sieve to get maximum texture, and stir the stock into the pan with the rabbit.

5 Bring the rabbit and sauce back to the boil, then simmer for 5–10 more minutes. Drizzle over the remaining olive oil and let the rabbit rest for half an hour before you eat it.

smoked eel with braised leeks

καπνιστό χέλι με πράσα

Early spring is the best time to go eel fishing in the delta of the Evros river, which is in north-eastern Greece up towards the Turkish border. As always with a seasonal glut, any way of preserving the surplus is welcome, and smoked eels become a valued addition to the storecupboard because they are so rich.

serves 6

2kg (4½lb) leeks, trimmed,
  washed well, and left whole
1 bunch spring onions, trimmed,
  washed well, and left whole
500g (18oz) small leafy carrots,
  trimmed, washed, and left whole
juice of 2 lemons
250ml (9fl oz) olive oil, plus extra
  for brushing
salt and pepper to taste
35g (1¼oz) bulgur
200g (7oz) prunes, stoned
1 bunch chives, finely chopped
500g (18oz) smoked eel in fillets
  (or smoked mackerel, which is a
  lot cheaper!)

to serve
lemon wedges
medium-hard feta cheese,
  crumbled

1 Place the leeks, spring onions, carrots, lemon juice, olive oil, and seasoning in a large saucepan. Put the lid on and turn the heat up to maximum for a couple of minutes, until the vegetables start boiling. Turn the temperature down to the lowest heat and cook until almost all the juices have gone and the leeks are tender – about an hour.

2 Add the bulgur, prunes, and 100ml (3½fl oz) water. Keep the pan not only over the low heat, but also in your mind, as the mixture will burn if you don't shake it every couple of minutes. Keep some more water handy in case you need to add it. Cook for 20–30 minutes, until all the water is absorbed and the oil remains. The vegetables will turn meltingly soft.

3 When the vegetables are ready, add the chives, remove the pan from the heat, and set aside with the lid on to cool.

4 Brush the eel fillets with a little olive oil and sear them in a ridged pan for 3 minutes on each side.

5 Serve the eel with the braised leeks, plenty of lemon wedges, and some feta cheese.

calf's tongue with okra

μοσχαρίσια γλώσσα με μπάμιες

On the face of it this dish sounds like a challenge, but persevere as the flavours and textures go well together. This is like a Greek cousin of the Irish dish crubeens, in that the meat is cooked and then fried in slices to give a contrasting texture.

serves 8

1 calf's tongue (ask your butcher to prepare it)

5 bay leaves

12 black peppercorns

6 garlic cloves

1 cinnamon stick

1kg (2¼lb) okra, the smallest you can find (about 3cm/1¼in)

3 bunches spring onions, trimmed and finely chopped

100g (3½oz) long, pale green peppers, seeded and thinly sliced

500g (18oz) plum tomatoes, peeled, seeded, and finely chopped

1 bunch flat-leaf parsley, finely chopped

salt and pepper to taste

150ml (5fl oz) olive oil

150g (5½oz) plain flour

3 eggs whisked with 1 tbsp milk (for egg wash)

150g (5½oz) fine breadcrumbs

olive oil for frying

thick Greek yoghurt, to serve

1 Put the whole tongue in a large pan and cover with water. Add the bay leaves, peppercorns, garlic, and cinnamon stick. Bring to the boil and simmer for about 2 hours, until the tongue is tender.

2 After about 45 minutes, preheat the oven to 200°C/400°F/gas mark 6.

3 Trim the stem ends of the okra without opening the pods. Spread them out in a single layer on a large roasting tray. Spread the spring onions, peppers and tomatoes over the okra and sprinkle with the parsley. Season well and pour over 100ml (3½fl oz) water and the olive oil. Bake for 40–60 minutes, until the okra are cooked but not mushy. Remove from the oven and allow to cool.

4 Take the tongue from the water and, while it is still hot, peel off the skin. Cut 1cm (½in) thick slices across the tongue. Season the flour, then use it to coat the slices. Dip them into the egg wash, and finally into the breadcrumbs.

5 Heat some olive oil and pan-fry the tongue slices for 1 minute on each side. Lay them on kitchen paper to absorb any excess oil and serve with the okra (which should be at room temperature) and 1 tbsp of yoghurt per portion.

pork and pickled cabbage casserole

χοιρινό κατσαρόλας με λάχανο τουρσί

This is a nostalgic dish for me – it always reminds me of my mother. To prepare it, you first have to make the lahano toursi *(a dish in its own right, see page 37), and that takes weeks. As soon as my mother started to make the pickled cabbage, the whole family knew that we would be getting this pork casserole in due course. My mother used to say that by the time the dish was in the pot our tongues had "marked the place where they had slept", which is a Greek expression roughly equivalent to saying that your "tongue is hanging out". It was always worth waiting for.*

serves 8

1 quantity *lahano toursi* (Greek pickled cabbage, see page 37)
125ml (4fl oz) olive oil
100g (3½oz) tomato *perasti* (the Greek equivalent of tomato passata)
1 tbsp sweet paprika
salt and pepper to taste
1 x 3kg (6½lb) pork shoulder joint, with the bone left in
140ml (4½fl oz) muscat wine
juice of 2 lemons

1 Soak the cabbage in water for 1–2 hours, changing the water several times, to desalt it. Drain well.

2 Heat the olive oil in a very large pot and add the cabbage. Mix with the tomato *perasti*, paprika, and seasoning, and cover. Let the cabbage soften in the oil on the heat for about 10 minutes.

3 Season the pork with salt and pepper.

4 Remove about half the cabbage from the pot and set aside. Place the pork in the pot on top of the cabbage and cover with the remaining cabbage. Pour in the muscat and lemon juice. Cover the pot and simmer for 2–2½ hours over a low heat, after which both the meat and the cabbage should be very tender. Add more muscat if the liquid runs dry. Check the seasoning. Be careful with the salt as we are using pickled cabbage.

5 Serve with saffron *hilopites* (see page 128).

men who fight, men who die

Inside every Greek there is a Spartan waiting to get out. In the same way that the modern-day Japanese revere the Samurai and seek to use their philosophy to solve modern-day problems, so Greeks will adopt a Spartan approach to negotiation, debate, and even cooking. The Spartan philosophy was one of the most rigorous belief systems ever invented. No wonder the city state of Sparta was more than a match for its northern rival, Athens, during the wars that rumbled on until the advent of Alexander the Great. Spartan principles make modern-day boot camps seem a soft option. The constant thread was the supremacy of the state over the individual, and that individual had one aim – to become a soldier. Literacy was not a part of Spartan education, for reading and writing played no role in a soldier's life. Nor were the arts a part of Spartan training. In fact the arts, with the exception of martial arts, were considered an obstacle to the development of military virtues. What was valued was silence, as expressed by stoicism in the face of suffering. Speaking briefly and to the point was greatly admired, and even today we call a terse individual 'laconic', in reference to the Spartan enclave of Laconia.

This hard line started at birth; mothers would not bathe the babies with water, but instead used wine, making bathtime the first test of their strength. Then, at the age of seven, boys were taken from their families to live apart in special "barracks" where they slept, ate, and were educated together. They were divided into age groups called "*agelai*" (which can be translated as "animals" or "flocks of animals"). Spartan children went barefoot and naked, and were given little food – this was to encourage them to forage for food, to live off the land or to steal. In Spartan society stealing was not looked down upon as being morally wrong, but getting caught was!

These Spartan attitudes have influenced many Greek dishes, particularly the food of the southern Peleponnese, where for some people food is not a joy, but rather a necessity. Food is seen as fuel rather than art, and so the less elaborate it is the better. Strangely these workmanlike dishes are not without charm, even though they are made with artisan ingredients such as the simple preserved meat *siglino* (a preserved pork). This principle even extends to *amyglalota*, which is a type of almond paste rather like marzipan – perfect as a way of storing the almond crop. For any "Spartan" (and remember that includes most Greeks, at least in their imagination), food brings with it a philosophical obligation – the food on the plate is set before us by God, so whatever your host offers you, you must eat rather than risk offending the Almighty. There's no room for sending back a steak to have it cooked more thoroughly or for turning down a nice piece of lightly charred liver. Spartan principles make a very good riposte to picky eaters!

belly pork with black-eye beans

χοιρινό με μαυρομάτικα φασόλια

I remember arriving at a mountain refuge high in the Taygetos mountains after a long day of cross-country skiing. There was a big pot on the fireplace containing a rich and satisfying stew of belly pork and black-eye beans for passing travellers. We ate it all and slept contented until the morning.

serves 4

1 tbsp cumin seeds

1 tbsp fennel seeds

1 x 1kg (2¼lb) piece of lean
  belly pork (get your butcher
  to bone it and take the rind off)

finely grated zest of 2 oranges

1 tbsp pickled green peppercorns

salt and pepper to taste

4 tbsp aged Corinthian red wine
  vinegar

9 tbsp olive oil

1 bunch coriander, finely chopped

black-eye beans

250g (9oz) black-eye beans,
  soaked overnight and rinsed

4 bay leaves

200g (7oz) carrots, finely chopped

2 celery sticks, finely chopped

1 bunch spring onions, finely
  chopped

1 Preheat the oven to 200°C/400°F/gas mark 6.

2 Dry-roast the cumin and fennel seeds in a frying pan.

3 Rub the inside part of the pork with the seeds and orange zest, and scatter evenly with the pickled green peppercorns. Roll up and secure with butcher's string.

4 Sprinkle the skin with salt and pepper, and roast the meat for about 1 hour and 20 minutes, until cooked through.

5 Meanwhile, place the beans in a saucepan with the bay leaves, carrots, celery and spring onions, cover with water and bring to the boil. Boil for 10 minutes, then turn the heat down and simmer – 45 minutes later the beans should be very soft. If they still have a bite, cook them for another 15 minutes. Drain the liquid, but do not discard it. Place the beans in a liquidizer and turn them into a fine purée. Add a little of the warm liquid to adjust the texture if required. Keep the purée somewhere warm.

6 When the pork is ready, remove it from the oven and let it rest for 15 minutes.

7 Reduce the red wine vinegar to half by boiling it in a hot, non-reactive pan. Prepare the dressing by adding the olive oil to the reduced vinegar.

8 Slice the pork roll thinly, drizzle over the dressing and serve with the bean purée and coriander.

calf's liver with rosemary

μοσχαρίσιο συκώτι με δεντρολίβανο

Rosemary is one of my mother's favourite high-summer flavourings. She has a small rosemary bush planted in the red soil of her garden and always says "You should never walk past a rosemary bush without running the leaves through your fingers and cutting a piece".

serves 4

200ml (7fl oz) olive oil

3 garlic cloves

½ bunch rosemary

75g (2¾oz) fine breadcrumbs

75g (2¾oz) plain flour

salt and pepper to taste

1kg (2¼lb) calf's liver (get your butcher to trim and slice it, ask for slices about 1cm/½in thick)

125ml (4fl oz) aged Corinthian red wine vinegar

to serve

country-style bread

1 Preheat your oven to 180°C/350°F/gas mark 4.

2 Put the olive oil, garlic, and rosemary into a small ovenproof pot, put the lid on, and place in the oven for 30–40 minutes. By then the oil should have taken up the flavours. Reserve the garlic.

3 Take 100ml (3½fl oz) of the infused oil and heat it in a frying pan. Mix the breadcrumbs and flour together, and season well.

4 Coat the liver slices in the flour and breadcrumbs, then pan-fry them a few at a time – it's best served pink. Place the cooked slices into a flat container – try to arrange them in a single layer.

5 When you have finished cooking the liver, pour all the hot oil into a container to cool down and wipe the bottom of the pan with kitchen paper. Put the pan back on the heat and deglaze with the red wine vinegar. Do not let the vinegar reduce. Add the unused remainder of the infused olive oil and whisk it for a minute. Add the reserved garlic cloves and finally pour all this over the liver.

6 This dish can be eaten straight away, but it will be even better a few hours later. Serve with country-style bread.

lahano toursi

λάχανο τουρσί

We all yearn for simple flavours and good seasonal dishes. For military cooks, this pickled cabbage provided a splendid source of vitamin C, while for the rest of us it has a grand, simple flavour. To make it you will either need a lahano *(a dense flat-headed cabbage available from Greek shops and other Mediterranean delicatessens) or a good, crisp British cabbage such as January King.*

serves 6

2kg (4½lb) "flat cabbage" (*lahano* preferably, or January King)
150g (5½oz) raw chickpeas
juice of 5 lemon, and finely grated zest of 4 lemons
150g (5½oz) sea salt

1　Take the heart of the flat-headed cabbage and separate it into individual leaves. Arrange the whole leaves in a large container (not aluminium) in layers, and between the layers sprinkle the chickpeas, lemon zest, and sea salt.

2　Pour over the lemon juice and top up the container with tap water. Place a couple of plates on the top to keep the cabbage submerged. Cover the container with a lid and refrigerate it unless you have a cool larder. Date it and reopen 4–6 weeks later.

3　Before eating, pick out the chickpeas – these are included to start the fermentation process, you don't eat them.

"For any 'Spartan' (and remember that includes most Greeks, at least in their imagination), food brings with it a philosophical obligation – the food on the plate is set before us by God, so whatever your host offers you, you must eat rather than risk offending the Almighty."

eggs with nettles and cheese

αυγά με τσουκνίδες και τυρί

When, as children, we were sent out to pick nettles, we had to wake up very early in the morning – before dawn, certainly before breakfast! My mother would answer our pleas for food by suggesting that we have a drink of water and so fool our stomachs into thinking that they had something to digest – it was her way of banishing hunger. First we would visit the sheep (it was lambing time), then collect the nettles, which had to be picked before the sun rose and made them wilt. If you are nettle-picking in Britain, you can have a bit of a lie-in as the British sun is unlikely to spoil them, but this is still a dish for spring, when the nettles are young and tender.

serves 4

500g (18oz) nettles (or 1kg/2¼lb green Swiss chard)
salt and pepper to taste
1 tbsp olive oil
15g (½oz) butter
150g (5½oz) *Xinomizithra* cheese (a soft cheese, mainly of sheep's milk) or ricotta
70g (2½oz) Greek yoghurt
4 eggs

to serve
country-style bread

1   Preheat the oven to 200°C/400°F/gas mark 6.

2   Blanch the nettles for 3–4 minutes in boiling salted water (wear rubber gloves while handling uncooked nettles). Roughly shred the cooked greens and taste for salt.

3   Heat the olive oil and butter together in an ovenproof pot, add the greens, and sauté for 5 minutes, stirring occasionally. Blend in the cheese and yoghurt.

4   Make four round "wells" in the greens, spacing them evenly. Break an egg into each and place the pot in the oven. Bake until the eggs are set – about 8–10 minutes. Season with salt and pepper.

5   Serve with plenty of good country-style bread.

yoghurt bread

γιαουρτόψωμο

*We Greeks see yoghurt as a key ingredient in many kinds of cooking –
it adds richness and a welcome tang. This bread will delight anyone who enjoys that slightly edgy
taste, similar to the one you get from traditional sourdough loaves.*

makes 2 plaited loaves

600g (1lb 5oz) strong white flour

2 eggs

125g (4½oz) Greek yoghurt

2 tsp salt

1 tbsp ground cinnamon

2 tsp white sugar

25g (1oz) fresh yeast

250ml (9fl oz) lukewarm milk

4 tbsp melted butter

1 egg mixed with 2 tbsp milk, for
   an egg wash

1   Put the flour, eggs, yoghurt, salt, cinnamon, sugar, fresh yeast and
lukewarm milk into the bowl of your food mixer. Using the dough hook
or kneading attachment, let the motor run on a low speed for 4 minutes
and then increase the speed. Add the melted butter and knead for
10 minutes.

2   Remove the bowl from the mixer, cover with a damp cloth and leave
in a warm place to prove for 1½ hours.

3   Knock the dough down by hand on a well-floured surface. Cut it
into six pieces (approximately 200g/7oz each) and plait them into two
loaves as you do for the *tsoureki* recipe (see page 108). Let the loaves
rest and prove for 30 minutes on a floured baking tray.

4   Preheat the oven to 220°C/425°F/gas mark 7.

5   Brush the tops of the loaves with egg wash and bake for 10 minutes,
then turn the temperature down to 180°C/350°F/gas mark 4 for a
further 20 minutes, or until cooked (the bread will sound hollow when
the base is tapped). Allow the bread to cool down before you cut it.

pastries, cakes and desserts

Greeks yield to no one in their love of all things sweet. While most people have a single "sweet tooth", we have several. Honey, sugar, and syrups play a big part in classic pastries such as *baklava, flogera,* and *bougatsa*. There are interesting desserts such as poached figs in red wine, two stunning ice-creams, plus a Greek coffee cake that can be served as a dessert or treat. Simpler but no less delicious, *svigi* is the Greek name for airy-light pancakes – easy to make and even easier to eat!

baklava

μπακλαβάς

Baklava should have 33 layers of filo, plus a reckless amount of butter. This number of leaves is supposed to reflect the fact that Christ lived on earth for 33 years. At first glance this recipe seems to use large quantities, but I urge you not to scale it down – when something is this good you should feast on it! Baklava is the nutty heart of our upbringing, a part of the way we are.

makes a roasting tray full

2 x 500g packets of ready-made
  filo (or make your own – see
  page 188 and stage 2 of method)
butter for greasing
whole cloves to decorate

filling

500g (18oz) walnut kernels,
  lightly roasted, then crushed
1 tbsp ground cinnamon
250g (9oz) caster sugar
450g (1lb) clarified butter (melted
  butter with creamy solids discarded)
150g (5½oz) fine semolina

syrup

250g (9oz) thyme honey
500g (18oz) sugar
500ml (18fl oz) water
finely grated zest of 2 lemons,
  plus juice of 1 lemon

1   To make the filling, mix the walnuts with the cinnamon and caster sugar, and reserve. Melt half the clarified butter in a saucepan and add the semolina. Coat the semolina in the butter without colouring it, then allow it to cool. Preheat your oven to 180°C/350°F/gas mark 4.

2   If making your own filo, double the quantities on page 188 and add 1 tsp of dried yeast to the dough; when it is ready, divide it into 33 before rolling each piece out. Butter a 30 x 15 x 5cm (12 x 6 x 2in) roasting dish. Arrange 10 filo sheets in it, buttering well as you add each one, and sprinkling with half the semolina. You'll need lots of butter.

3   Add a layer made up of half the walnut and cinnamon mixture, then layer another 10 filo sheets on top, buttering and adding semolina as before. Add another layer using the remaining walnut mix. Layer the remaining filo sheets on top, using just as much butter as before.

4   With a sharp knife, score the top of the *baklava*: you should be cutting through the top six sheets to mark out portions. Decorate each portion by pinning it with a clove. Spray with water and put in the oven for 30 minutes. Turn the oven down to 140°C/275°F/gas mark 1, and continue baking for 2–2½ hours. The top of the *baklava* should stay golden (not dark brown). Remove from the oven and allow to cool.

5   Put all the ingredients for the syrup except the lemon juice in a pan and bring to the boil. When the syrup just coats the back of a spoon, add the lemon juice and, while it is still hot, pour it over the cold *baklava*. Leave to rest overnight, and the next day indulge yourself.

flogera and bougatsa

φλογέρα και μπουγάτσα

As we left the hotel after overnighting in Thessaloniki, my father always insisted we ate no breakfast. He planned to stop at the bakery and buy us a portion of bougatsa. *This is a kind of custard slice and comes in an elegant paper envelope with a little extra cinnamon and icing sugar sprinkled on the cut edge.* Flogera *is made from the same pastry and custard filling.*

makes enough flogera *for a party, or 1 large* bougatsa

custard filling

1 vanilla pod
325ml (11fl oz) full-fat milk
325ml (11fl oz) double cream
finely grated zest of 1 orange
3 egg yolks
175g (6oz) caster sugar
70g (2½oz) semolina

flogera

250g (9oz) clarified butter
16 sheets of filo pastry
   (30 x 15cm) (see page 188)
1 quantity of custard filling
250ml (9fl oz) of Metaxa syrup
   (see page 62)

bougatsa

150g (5½oz) clarified butter
12 filo sheets (30 x 15cm)
1 quantity of custard filling
icing sugar
ground cinnamon

1   First make the custard filling. Split the vanilla pod lengthways and strip the seeds into the milk in a saucepan. Add the cream and orange zest and warm, but do not allow the mixture to get hotter than 60°C/140°F.

2   In a mixing bowl, add the yolks to the caster sugar and whisk until you have a very fluffy white cream. Continue whisking slowly as you add the warm milk. Add the semolina and whisk for a further 2 minutes.

3   Place the bowl over simmering water and stir constantly, as the semolina is heavy and will sit at the bottom of the bowl. Keep an eye on the temperature, as it must not exceed 70°C/158°F. When it's ready and has a texture like heavy custard, take off the heat. Cool, then refrigerate.

flogera

1   Using the clarified butter, butter the filo well. Put the custard in a piping bag and spread a 16th along the edge of the 15cm length of each sheet. Fold in the edges to enclose the filling, then butter and roll. Keep buttering and rolling until you have a 15cm sausage. Do not be put off by the amount of butter you use, as it will prevent leakage.

2   Preheat the oven to 180°C/350°F/gas mark 4. Line a baking sheet with a sheet of oven parchment. Arrange the *flogeres* on this and spray them with water. Bake for 15–20 minutes – they should get some colour, but the filo should not be crispy. Remove from the oven and place them in a shallow container in which they fit snugly. Pour the syrup (at room temperature) over them. Ideally you should eat them warm, but they will keep in a refrigerator for up to 3 days.

flogeres

bougatsa

1 Using the clarified butter, butter a rectangular roasting dish (30 x 15 x 5cm) well. Preheat the oven to 180°C/350°F/gas mark 4.

2 Roll out your filo sheets to the same dimensions as the tray. Line the base of the tray with half the filo (roughly six sheets), buttering each sheet well before you add the next. Spread with the custard filling. Top with the remaining filo, buttering well as per the base.

3 Spray the top of the *bougatsa* with water and bake for 30 minutes. It is ready when the top is golden and is starting to flake; the fillings should be firm, but not hard. Remove from the oven and sprinkle with icing sugar and cinnamon. Cut into squares and serve at room temperature. Do not reheat.

greek coffee cake

κέικ με γεύση ελληνικού καφέ

This is not the kind of cake you find in Greek pastry shops, but was a speciality of my mother's, who would bake it for important dinner parties. My father's shop had a seemingly inexhaustible supply of wonderful Manouri cheese. He used to describe this cake as "Halandri meets Detroit" – Halandri being his birthplace and Detroit my mother's.

makes 1 deep 20cm (8in) cake

250g (9oz) self-raising flour

3 eggs, separated

250g (9oz) caster sugar

150g (5½oz) unsalted butter

2 tsp extra virgin olive oil

2 tbsp Greek coffee (either made the traditional way, or whatever method you use, but using finely ground Greek coffee)

6 tbsp full-fat milk

butter for greasing

filling

300g (10½oz) room temperature Manouri cheese (or cream cheese)

finely grated zest of 1 lemon

finely grated zest of 3 mandarins or clementines

300g (10½oz) icing sugar

3 tbsp Greek coffee (see above)

1   Preheat your oven to 180°C/350°F/gas mark 4.

2   Sift the flour into a mixing bowl. Beat the egg yolks, caster sugar, butter, and olive oil together in a separate bowl until you get a white fluffy cream (you can use a food processor). Add the flour while mixing, then blend in the coffee and milk.

3   In a different bowl, whisk the egg whites to soft peaks. Stir a bit of the whites into the cake mixture before folding the rest through.

4   Butter 2 x 20cm (8in) cake tins and divide the mixture equally between them. Bake for approximately 40–50 minutes. The cakes are cooked when their centre is springy. Unmould them and place them on a wire rack to cool completely.

5   To make the filling, put the Manouri cheese and the two different zests in a bowl and mix together with a hand blender. Slowly add the icing sugar and wait until each addition has worked in completely before adding any more. The final result will be a thick paste. Finally, beat in the coffee until that is incorporated too.

6   Spread a generous third of the filling on one of the cakes, then place the second cake on the top. Cover the top and sides of the cake with the remaining filling using a palette knife.

diples

δίπλες

At home we only make diples *at Christmas. They are time-consuming and necessitate a family production line: some people rolling out the dough, some forming the* diples, *some frying, and some dipping them in syrup. We would make a mountain of them, but they always seemed to run out in double-quick time.*

makes about 50 diples

6 whole eggs plus 6 egg whites
finely grated zest and juice of
  2 organic or unwaxed oranges
½ tsp bicarbonate of soda
½ tsp salt
about 900g (2lb) self-raising flour

syrup
600g (1lb 5oz) Greek honey

to finish
vegetable oil for deep-frying
2 tbsp ground cinnamon
400g (14oz) shelled walnuts,
  crushed and toasted

1 Whisk the whole eggs, orange juice, zest, bicarbonate of soda, and salt together well.

2 Start adding the flour, up to about 700g (1lb 9oz) to begin with, until you can't whisk it any longer because the mixture is reaching the consistency of dough. From this point start using your hands and work until the dough becomes smooth and not sticky.

3 Whisk the egg whites until they are the consistency of soft meringue. Mix them into the dough. You will then need to add more flour (use the remaining 200g/7oz) and knead until you have a silky dough. Wrap the dough in clingfilm and leave to rest for at least 30 minutes.

4 Make the syrup by heating the honey and 300ml (10fl oz) water together until they have combined, then cooling to room temperature.

5 If you have a pasta machine, roll the dough in long, thin strips, 20 x 5cm (8 x 2in). Otherwise use a rolling pin and roll the dough as fine as you can before cutting into strips. Dampen the short edges and seal to make large rings.

6 Heat the vegetable oil to 150°C/300°F. Fry the *diples* a few at a time until crisp. Drain on kitchen paper. When cool enough to handle, dip them in the syrup, then sprinkle plenty of toasted crushed walnuts and cinnamon over them. Keep any spare syrup to "refresh" the *diples*, which should last into a second day.

rizogalo

ρυζόγαλο

Most people who have holidayed in Greece have come home with tales of rice pudding. They are usually slightly puzzled by our national obsession with such a simple dish, and many do not try rizogalo simply because it is subtitled rice pudding and they have been put off by school-dinner stodge in their youth. The best rizogalo is a delight: creamy and yet with a subtle bite to each grain. It is like a sophisticated dessert risotto.

serves 4

150g (5½oz) short-grain
   pudding rice
600ml (1 pint) full-fat milk
140g (5oz) sugar
30g (1¼oz) cornflour
3 egg yolks
ground cinnamon

1 Place the rice in a saucepan with 300ml (10fl oz) water. Cook over low heat, stirring continuously.

2 Put the milk in a second saucepan with half the sugar and warm it through, stirring. By now the rice should have absorbed all the water (this takes approximately 10 minutes).

3 Add the warm milk to the rice and continue cooking for about 20 minutes. Keep the lid on and the heat very low, and stir from time to time.

4 Mix the cornflour with 2 tbsp water until you have a sloppy paste and stir this into the rice. Leave it to simmer for 5 minutes while it thickens. Remove the saucepan from the heat, put the lid on, and leave it to rest for 10 minutes.

5 Whisk the egg yolks with the remaining sugar and add to the *rizogalo* mix. The heat should be between 65°C and 80°C (149–176°F): this is critical, too low and it will not thicken, and too high will mean scrambled egg!

6 Serve with plenty of ground cinnamon. *Rizogalo* tastes better when is eaten at room temperature.

Note: At the restaurant we make the *rizogalo* slightly moodier by crushing 4 little lumps of mastic with 1 tsp of sugar, then adding it to the rice in stage 1. This gives a wonderfully exotic flavour.

an evening stroll
to the pastry shop

There's no doubt about it, we Greeks are different to the rest of you. We certainly have a different attitude to desserts and sweets. For most northern Europeans, sweets are seen as a treat. English kids are told that if they eat up their greens they will get something sweet for pudding. Parisian children are sent out to the *pâtisserie* to fetch home a perfect strawberry tart, every glistening berry immaculate, which then becomes the grand finale of a formal dinner. For Greeks, sweet things to eat are a much more mainstream affair: for a start we are most likely to eat sweets early in the morning on the way to school or work; or with a coffee after a siesta; or just whenever we fancy something sweet – which is nearly all the time! In that respect we Greeks line up with our neighbours in the Middle East – we like sweet things a lot.

Pick any day to wander into the kitchen and open the door of my mother's refrigerator, and you'll find the desserts lined up and waiting. There may be a dozen small bowls of *ryzogalo* flavoured subtly with mastic, or a row of rich cinnamon custards neatly portioned out, or a tray of pastries soaked in honey. These goodies are not reserved for a special occasion, but are an important part of everyday living. If your sweet tooth insists that it's time for something sweet to eat, then it would be downright rude to make it wait through a few *mezedes* and a nice piece of fish and some cheese before getting to the point. In a Greek household, you are much more likely to be offered a glass of sweet wine and a piece of fruit than a conventional "pudding" course. Desserts and pastries are for enjoying.

In our house the only exception to these principles was ice-cream, which for some inexplicable reason seemed linked with Sunday. We always had ice-cream on summer sundays. But once again the Greek way is slightly different and you would always make a rich but plain ice-cream then top it with a specially made sweet syrup, or bottled fruit, or *glykos*, which are like superior-quality jams that are eaten straight off the spoon as an accompaniment to coffee. The ice-cream is in a strictly supporting role to provide a cool counterpoint to the really sweet stuff.

Each and every year my father would take the family on a trip to taste the new season's cheeses in western Macedonia before placing orders for his shop. He always arranged for us to spend a full day in Thessaloniki to sample the famous pastries and revitalize our tastebuds after all that strong cheese. Ever since these trips I have associated Thessaloniki with the best pastries and spectacular sunsets. Thessaloniki is Greece's second-largest city and the nearest thing we have to a university town such as Oxford or Cambridge. Having plenty of students means plenty of cafés, and the local custom is to take a stroll in the warmth of the evening and watch the sun go down. There is a famous promenade by the White Tower that is lined with cafés where they are only too happy to leave you alone with your thoughts, a strong coffee and a sweet pastry. Whether you people-watch – sit long enough and it seems as if the whole town will stroll by – or concentrate on the sun dipping into the Aegean is up to you.

Among Athenian society Thessaloniki has a reputation for being a rather raffish and bohemian city. Perhaps this is due to the student population, or perhaps it is because the city is home to all the best Greek *rebetiko* singers (a kind of "jazz/folk"). This is a strange kind of music, often sad, and a genre where the meaning of the lyrics and nuance of the interpretation are crucial. Another key influence has been the arrival over the years of waves of incomers. Thessaloniki has become home to a substantial Jewish population, both the Ashkenazi from Central Europe and the Sephardim from Iberia and Italy. It also became a refuge for large numbers of the "Greek minority" when they were forced to leave Eastern Turkey in 1922. All these exotic stimuli have helped shape attitudes to pastries and desserts. So it seems perfectly in keeping to see rows of small baker's shops vying with one another to prepare the perfect *baklava*; or *flogera*, those long, delicate filo parcels filled with a rich custard which are named after the flutes whose shape they resemble. Then first thing in the morning the identical shops will be selling *bougatsa*, a pastry that is made up from the same elements as *flogera,* but that comes in chunky slices with a heavy dusting of sugar – the perfect finger food for eating on the way to lectures or work.

For me there will always be two perfect places to eat desserts: on the seafront at Thessaloniki while watching the sun going down, and anywhere else you care to mention!

pancakes

τηγανίτες

When we were children hanging around the kitchen, if my mother wanted to get rid of us she used to make these quick and easy pancakes called "svigi". We were allowed to choose between savoury and sweet. If there were a lot of people at home in the early evening, there would be a queue in the kitchen for a fresh pancake straight from the pan to go with a glass of mountain dark tea or dessert wine.

makes about 20 pancakes

70g (2½oz) "00" type flour (also
   known as pasta flour)
4 eggs
400g (14oz) strained yoghurt
½ bunch mint, finely chopped
finely grated zest of 1 lemon
½ tsp bicarbonate of soda
1 tbsp groundnut oil
15g (½oz) unsalted butter

1　Put the flour in a mixing bowl.

2　In another bowl, or jug, beat together the eggs and yoghurt. Add the mint, lemon zest, and bicarbonate of soda. Work the liquid into the flour with a wooden spoon until you have a stiff batter. If it looks too runny, add a little more flour. Only practice will make perfect!

3　Grease the pan with a little oil and butter. Cook spoonfuls of the mixture on both sides (turn them or toss them when they are risen and golden on one side).

4　Remove from the oil and use your imagination to decide on the topping: honey, cinnamon, and nuts; preserved fruits and Manouri cheese; room-temperature soft cheese with black pepper; crushed summery tomatoes with olive oil, herbs, olives, and feta; or simply serve with ice-cream and preserved sour cherries.

karydopita

καρυδόπιτα

This tray bake tastes terrific. It is a winter cake and my mother would refuse to make it after Easter, as she believed that the walnuts were no longer at their best and preferred to wait for the new season's crop to come round again. As children, when we fought our punishment would often be "Go and shell a bucket of walnuts!".

fills 1 large roasting dish

70g (2½oz) butter, plus extra for greasing

150g (5½oz) caster sugar

3 eggs, separated

70g (2½oz) self-raising flour

70g (2½oz) semolina

1 tsp ground cinnamon

140g (5oz) shelled walnut halves, half very finely chopped

4 tbsp full-fat milk

1 quantity Metaxa syrup (see page 62), at room temperature

1 Preheat the oven to 180°C/350°F/gas mark 4, and lightly butter a roasting dish of about 24 x 12 x 5cm (9½ x 4½ x 2in).

2 Cream the butter and sugar together in a large mixing bowl, then beat in the egg yolks. Whisk until light and fluffy (you could use an electric mixer for this). Add the flour, semolina, and cinnamon, and mix well. This makes a heavy mixture if your electric mixer cannot cope, add some of the milk. Switch to mixing by hand, and add all the walnuts and either all or the remaining milk.

3 Whisk the egg whites in another bowl until they form stiff peaks.

4 Fold the egg whites gently into the main mixture. Stir, but do not beat the air out of the mixture. Empty the mix into the roasting dish and bake for 45–50 minutes. You can tell whether the cake is ready by testing it with a skewer: when the skewer comes out clean, the cake is cooked.

5 Leave the cake in its tray and, while it is still hot, pour the Metaxa syrup over the top and allow to soak in for 2 hours before cutting. Keep the tray flat or all the syrup will run up to one end.

figs poached in red wine

συκαλάκια Κύμης με κόκκινο κρασί

In Greece, many households have a fig tree in the courtyard, and fresh figs are a daily treat when in season. This means that to be sought after, dried figs have to be of superlative quality. The dried figs from Kimi are highly prized and rarely seem to go "crystalline". These poached figs go well with the Manouri terrine (see page opposite), but Greeks love them as a topping for vanilla or chocolate ice-cream, or with plenty of coarse black pepper as an accompaniment to feta cheese.

serves 8

500g (18oz) "ready to eat" dried
   figs (from Kimi if possible)

1 x 75cl bottle red wine

55g (2oz) thyme honey

25g (1oz) caster sugar

2 vanilla pods

2 cinnamon sticks

1 The "ready to eat" figs are best because they need less rehydration. Cut each fig in half lengthways and place in a non-reactive saucepan with all the remaining ingredients.

2 Bring them to simmering point and continue simmering until the liquid has been reduced by half and is just thick enough to coat the back of a spoon.

3 The figs will keep for up to 3 weeks in a clean jar.

"...once again the Greek way is slightly different and you would always make a rich but plain ice-cream and then top it with a specially made sweet syrup, or bottled fruit, or glykos, which are like superior-quality jams that are eaten straight off the spoon as an accompaniment to coffee."

manouri terrine

μανούρι "παγωτό"

Manouri is a splendid soft cheese, which is made using mainly ewes'
milk. It is more savoury than Italian mascarpone, but that is the only substitute cheese that comes
close. Manouri is not for the cheese board, but goes well with peppers, or even poached fruits. My
mother used to slice a fresh fig in half then sandwich it back together with Manouri in the middle.

serves 8

250ml (9fl oz) full-fat milk
125ml (4fl oz) double cream
350g (12oz) Manouri cheese
500g (18oz) figs poached in red
  wine (see opposite), drained
coarsely ground black pepper
aged Corinthian red wine vinegar
  (or balsamic vinegar)

1 Put the milk, cream, and Manouri cheese in a large saucepan and
heat through very gently. After approximately 40 minutes the cheese
will have melted into the milk. Do not be put off by the fact that it
looks curdled. Set it aside.

2 Place 400g (14oz) of the poached figs in a processor and blend until
you have a coarse, crunchy paste. If your processor is not powerful
enough to blitz the figs, help it along by adding some of the fig juices.
While the machine is running, add the cheese mixture and process
until smooth.

3 Let the mixture cool down, then churn it in an ice-cream machine
for about 30 minutes if you have a large machine or in smaller batches
if appropriate to your machine – stop while the mixture is still soft. If
you do not have an ice-cream machine, pour the mixture into a tray and
place in the freezer; after 10 minutes, stir thoroughly to break up the
ice crystals; after another 10 minutes, stir again – continue freezing and
stirring until the ice-cream is cold, but still soft.

4 Pour half the mixture into a terrine dish approximately 30 x 10 x 8cm
(12 x 4 x 3¼in). Lay the remainder of the figs on the top, sprinkle over
some coarsely ground black pepper, and top with the remaining
mixture. Cover and place in the freezer. Do not eat on the same day.

5 To serve, cut into slices with a warm knife. To decorate the plate,
make a simple sauce by reducing some vinegar by half, then cooling.

preserved sour cherries

βύσσινο γλυκό

*This is one of a class of Greek treats called "glykos" ("spoon sweets",
so-called because you eat them with a spoon). But the preserved cherries are versatile and also make a
refreshing drink. Mix a couple of spoons of the cherry preserve with water, plenty of ice, and lemon
slices in a tall glass, and stir well. This was a treat for us during the hot days of summer.*

fills 4–5 450g (1lb) jars

1kg (2¼lb) sour cherries (or
  ordinary cherries)
1kg (2¼lb) sugar

1   The most time-consuming part of this recipe is the first step –
pitting the cherries!

2   Put the pitted cherries and sugar in a saucepan and cook over a low
heat. Do not worry about the absence of water. The sugar will soon start
to melt: as it does so, keep skimming the surface to remove any scum.

3   The preserve is ready when the syrup is thick enough to coat the
back of a spoon.

4   Put it in clean sterilized jars with close-fitting lids while still hot.

halva

χαλβάς κατσαρόλας

When we were children, we were not allowed our own glass of dessert wine, but we could dip biscuits, or delicacies such as halva, into our father's glass. This meant that in our family halva was made in a long, long sausage about 5cm (2in) across. Sometimes we would make 4 metres of halva – my mother has a huge kitchen with long, cool marble worktops – but it is a lot easier to aim for 4 sausages about 25cm (10in) long.

makes about 40 roundels

60g (2¼oz) butter

100g (3½oz) shelled pistachios, crushed

55g (2oz) semolina

55g (2oz) polenta

375ml (13fl oz) full-fat milk, hot but not boiling

syrup

finely grated zest and juice of 1 orange and 1 lemon

75g (2¾oz) Greek thyme honey

60g (2¼oz) caster sugar

1 cinnamon stick

1 Make the syrup by heating all the ingredients together with 375ml (13fl oz) water in a pan. Stir, bring to the boil, and reduce by roughly half (you should have about 250ml/9fl oz) before turning off the heat.

2 In a large pot, melt the butter and toss in the pistachios. Add the semolina and polenta, and stir for a few minutes until everything is coated in butter, but not coloured or burned.

3 Start adding the syrup slowly, slowly, as if you were making risotto, and stir with a wooden spoon. Be very careful because, as you pour the syrup into the pot, the liquid will start spattering. Keep stirring.

4 When all the syrup has been used, start adding the hot milk a bit at a time. By this stage you will feel fairly exhausted, but keep stirring! When all the milk has been worked into the mixture, take the pot off the heat and put the lid on. Let it cool down completely. As you lift the lid you should get a delicious, citrussy smell.

5 Take a long sheet of parchment paper and spread the mixture on the paper. Roll it firmly, so you end up with long, condensed cylinders – four, of about 25cm (10in) long. Leave in the refrigerator to set firmly. Cut into discs to serve.

6 Eat the *halva*, either on its own with sprinkled icing sugar and ground cinnamon, or with Metaxa and sultana ice-cream (see page 63) or some lime syrup (see page 62).

lime syrup

σιρόπι μοσχολέμονου

This syrup has a wide variety of uses – you can poach fruits in it, pour it over ice-cream, or soak cakes and pastries in it.

Makes about 300ml (10fl oz)

finely grated zest and juice of
  7 limes
500g (18oz) white sugar
2 bay leaves
2 cinnamon sticks

1   Place all the ingredients in a non-reactive saucepan with 500ml (18fl oz) of water, stir, then bring the mixture to a boil. Simmer, skimming as necessary to remove scum.

2   When the liquid is reduced by half, remove from the heat and cool. The syrup should be a pretty pale-green colour. Strain. The syrup will keep well in a clean, sterilized jar, and does not need to be refrigerated.

metaxa syrup

σιρόπι Μεταξά

Metaxa is one of the classic flavours of Greece. This syrup is most useful for adding character to all manner of desserts and pastries.

Makes about 300ml (10fl oz)

250g (9oz) white sugar
55g (2oz) thyme honey
100ml (3½fl oz) Metaxa brandy

1   Place the sugar, honey and 185ml (6¼fl oz) of water in a saucepan, stir, then bring the mixture to a boil.

2   Skim as necessary to remove scum. When the liquid is reduced by 25 per cent, add the Metaxa and boil for another 2 minutes. Remove from the heat and cool down. The syrup keeps well in a clean, sterilized jar, and does not need to be refrigerated.

metaxa and sultana ice-cream

παγωτό με σταφίδα και μπράντυ μεταξά

*This is a glorious and sloppy ice-cream. Do not hope for it to freeze
rock hard as the addition of the Metaxa means an alcohol level that makes this virtually impossible.*

makes about 1.25 litres (2 pints)

500ml (18fl oz) full-fat milk

500ml (18fl oz) double cream

7 egg yolks (8 if using small eggs)

150g (5½oz) caster sugar

50ml (2fl oz) Metaxa brandy

125g (4½oz) brandy-soaked
    sultanas (see note)

sultanas

500g (18oz) sultanas (the plump
    ones from Corinth are best)

200ml (7fl oz) Metaxa brandy

1   Put the milk and cream in a saucepan and heat until warm – the
temperature should be 55°C/130°F.

2   Put the egg yolks in a mixing bowl and add the sugar. With a hand
blender, whisk until you've got a white, creamy texture.

3   Reduce the speed of the blender to the minimum and start pouring
the warm milk and cream into the bowl. Continue, slowly, until it is all
used up. Place the mixing bowl over a pan of simmering water and keep
stirring until you've got full-bodied custard. Do not allow the
temperature to exceed 70°C/158°F or the mixture will curdle.

4   Remove the custard from the heat and place the bowl in a large
container with ice.

5   When the custard is thoroughly cool, pour into your ice-cream
machine, adding the brandy. After the machine has been running for
15 minutes, add the sultanas. When the texture is soft but not runny,
serve or pack into a tub and store in the freezer.

6   If you do not have an ice-cream machine, pour the mixture into a
tray and place in the freezer. After 10 minutes, stir thoroughly to break
up the ice crystals. After another 10 minutes, stir while adding the
brandy. After another 10 minutes stir and add the sultanas. Continue
freezing and stirring until the ice-cream is ready.

Note: My mother always keeps a jar of brandy-soaked sultanas in the
cupboard. They make a splendid garnish for all sorts of desserts and
will taste their best after two weeks. Mix the sultanas and brandy in a
preserving jar, put the lid on, give it a shake, and keep.

greek coffee ice-cream

παγωτό με γεύση ελληνικού καφέ

In our household, ice-creams were a predictable if delicious sweet. In the winter, my mother would make chocolate or vanilla ice-cream; in the summer, chocolate, vanilla, apricot, peach, or strawberry. Greek ice-cream parlours, however, sell tonnes of mocha ice-cream. Why they don't make it with Greek coffee is a mystery. Serve this ice-cream with either preserved sour cherries (see page 58) or chocolate truffles (see page 22).

makes 1.25 litres (2 pints)

55g (2oz) ground Greek coffee
500ml (18fl oz) full-fat milk
500ml (18fl oz) double cream
150g (5½oz) caster sugar
7 egg yolks (8 if small eggs)

1 First make the Greek coffee. If you haven't got a small traditional copper pot to make it on the stove top, make it using your usual method. Greek coffee is very finely ground and its silt-like texture contributes to the texture of the ice-cream. You need to end up with 175ml (6fl oz) of Greek coffee.

2 Pour the milk and cream into a saucepan and warm them through to about 55°C/130°F. Pour the coffee into the warm milk and cream.

3 In a mixing bowl, whisk the sugar with the egg yolks until you've got a white, creamy texture. Continue whisking as you add the warm milk and coffee mixture to the bowl.

4 Place the mixing bowl over a pan of simmering water and keep stirring until you've got a custard that coats the back of a spoon. Do not allow the temperature to exceed 70°C/158°F.

5 Remove the custard from the heat and allow to cool down. When it is thoroughly cold, pour into your ice-cream machine. When the texture is soft but not runny, serve or pack into a tub and store in the freezer.

6 If you do not have an ice-cream machine, pour the mixture into a tray and place in the freezer. After 10 minutes, stir thoroughly to break up the ice crystals. Then stir again after every 10 minutes. Continue freezing and stirring until the ice-cream is ready.

harvest home

As Greek cooking is so tightly bound up with the changing seasons, harvest time means both hard work and a chance to enjoy a glut of produce at its best. This chapter includes some splendid tomato recipes – for instance, a tomato soup with yoghurt and classic stuffed tomatoes – a special *dolmades*, and some splendid dishes made with capers. Then there are staples such as *keftedakia*: simple meatballs, just the thing to refuel hungry grape-pickers.

tomato keftedes

ντοματοκεφτέδες σαντορίνης

For four stunning weeks after the day of the Virgin Mary on August 15th, tomatoes become an obsession on Santorini. They are sun ripened and packed with flavour. Eat these tomato keftedes *hot – the flavour will explode in your mouth.*

makes 10 keftedes

20 small tomatoes, rinsed and dried

sea salt

1 bunch thyme, leaves only

½ recipe quantity batter (see page 187)

½ bunch mint, finely chopped

½ bunch chervil, finely chopped

1 bunch flat-leaf parsley, finely chopped

1 bunch chives, finely chopped

2 bunches spring onions, finely chopped

2 tbsp olive oil

salt and pepper to taste

groundnut oil for frying

1   Preheat the oven to the lowest possible heat. Cut the tomatoes in half, place them on rack in a roasting dish and sprinkle with plenty of sea salt and thyme. In an ideal world you put them in the sun for couple of days until ready, but you'll probably have to make do with putting them in the oven overnight. The next day they should be ready.

2   Make the batter and leave to stand in a mixing bowl.

3   Mix the herbs and spring onion with the oil and season. Combine two pieces of tomato with 1 dsp of herbs and 1 dsp of batter and form into a flat cake. Repeat to make 10 cakes.

4   Pour the groundnut oil into a large frying pan to a depth of about 2.5cm (1in). When it is hot but not smoking, fry the *keftedes* in the hot oil. Turn the tomato *keftedes* over, cooking until lightly golden all over.

tomato soup with yoghurt

ντοματόσουπα με στραγγισμένο γιαούρτι του Ρούσσα

The 6th December is Saint Nicolas's Day, an important Greek national holiday. Because my father is an atheist, rather than allowing us to get involved with the festivities, he would send us off to a village in Western Macedonia to spend the day with a sheep farmer. I learned a lot about sheep, but even more about yoghurt. Greek yoghurt is made from sheep's milk, which has a fat content of 10 per cent, whereas cow's milk yoghurt has only 4 per cent fat. In the restaurant we use a traditional sheep's milk yoghurt. The taste of Greek yoghurt changes with the seasons because milk is richer in fat in the winter than it is in summer. The most delicious yoghurt is "strained yoghurt", which is used to make genuine tzatziki. Once the yoghurt sets, it is stirred, placed in cheesecloth, and left to hang for 12 hours. This drains off all the excess water, and the resulting yoghurt is firm enough to be sold by weight.

serves 6

200ml (7fl oz) extra virgin
  olive oil
500g (18oz) button onions
2kg (4½lb) fresh tomatoes,
  skinned, seeded and very
  finely chopped
150g (5½oz) *trahanas* (a kind of
  tiny pasta about the size of a
  pine needle; you can substitute
  coarse bulgur)
salt and pepper to taste
300g (10½oz) strained Greek-
  style yoghurt
a few fresh mint leaves for garnish

1 Heat the olive oil in a large saucepan, then sweat the button onions for 5 minutes with the lid on.

2 Add the tomatoes and bring to the boil. As the mixture boils, skim off any impurities during the first 5 minutes.

3 There is a secret to cooking *trahanas* so that you get the classic sloppy texture. You need seven parts liquid to one part *trahanas*. Judge the quantities by eye and add boiling water to the tomato and onion pot as necessary. When you have the right amount of liquid, add the *trahanas*. This works for bulgur as well.

4 Simmer over a low heat for about 45 minutes, until the soup is thick and the *trahanas* or bulgur is soft. Adjust the seasoning.

5 Serve in individual bowls, adding a large dollop of strained yoghurt in the middle and garnishing with fresh mint leaves.

caper and tomato giahni

κάπαρη Σαντορίνης γιαχνί

I remember sailing away from Santorini in October, with dishes such as this imprinted on my memory. This recipe sums up the strong, rich flavours of autumn: concentrated tomato and onion flavours are balanced by the tang of capers.

serves 4

100ml (3½fl oz) olive oil

500g (18oz) button onions

8 garlic cloves

1 x 400g jar Greek tomato *perasti*
(the Greek equivalent of tomato passata)

150g brined capers, strained

black pepper

1 Heat the olive oil, then sweat the whole onions and garlic cloves over a very low heat with the lid on until soft – about 20–30 minutes.

2 When the onions are softened but not browned, add the tomato *perasti* and continue cooking, but not for more than 10 minutes, as the tomatoes can turn a bit acidic.

3 Stir in the capers and remove from the heat. Let the pan rest on a cooling rack for a couple of hours. The longer it rests the better it will taste, as the flavour of the capers will mingle with the other ingredients. Add plenty of coarsely ground black pepper – you are unlikely to need any salt because of the capers.

Tomato perasti: In this book there are several references to "tomato *perasti*". When my friend and supplier of Greek produce, Panagiotis Manuelidis, first brought a jar of tomato *perasti* into the kitchen for us to try, we were amazed by the intensity of its flavour. Panagiotis has persuaded a tomato grower in Greece to pass his entire crop through a vegetable mouli, remove all the watery juices and bottle it. That's it! No chemicals added. This means that we have got plenty of tomatoes to use during the months when the sun is too weak to ripen and flavour tomatoes. By the end of September we need to find space in the restaurant stores for enough jars to last the winter – 10,000 of them! Tomato *perasti* is passata with character. You'll find it under the Odysea brand in an increasing number of good supermarkets.

stuffed tomatoes

λαδερές ντομάτες γεμιστές

At home, this dish came to the table on hot Sundays as we returned from the sea, but it was also served at lavish dinners when my mother wanted to satisfy her desire for ostentation. It proved equally popular in either type of meal.

serves 12

12 large tomatoes (select really
    big ones)

salt and pepper to taste

250g (9oz) white onions, finely
    chopped

55g (2oz) pine nuts

300ml (10fl oz) olive oil

250g (9oz) short- or medium-
    grain rice, washed and drained

55g (2oz) sultanas (from Corinth
    preferably)

1 bunch flat-leaf parsley, finely
    chopped

500g (18oz) potatoes

1   Slice the tops off the tomatoes and reserve to use as lids. Remove and discard the seeds, then scoop out the pulp and put it in a bowl. Salt and pepper the insides of the hollow tomatoes and put in a roasting tray.

2   Wash the onions and drain in a colander – this will make the onions taste less assertive. Toss the pine nuts in a hot, dry frying pan until toasted – 2–3 minutes. Preheat your oven to 180°C/350°F/gas mark 4.

3   Heat 100ml (3½fl oz) of the olive oil in a saucepan, then brown the onion. Add the rice, sultanas and toasted pine nuts. Stir and mix well, then add the tomato pulp, salt, pepper, parsley, and 250ml (9fl oz) of water, and simmer until the rice is half cooked – about 10 minutes.

4   With a small spoon, fill each tomato case with the mixture, remembering to allow room for the rice to expand (it is only half cooked). Cover the filled tomatoes with their tops.

5   Clean, wash and cut the potatoes into wedges, salt and pepper them and place them between the tomatoes. Pour the remaining olive oil over the tomatoes and potatoes, and bake for 45–60 minutes.

6   Allow to cool and serve at room temperature.

caper dip

ντιπ κάπαρης

This creamy dip, which has much the same look and consistency as mayonnaise, goes well with either poached fish or boiled eggs.

makes about 400ml (14fl oz)

100g (3½oz) day-old stale bread

100g (3½oz) brined capers, rinsed and drained

1 bunch flat-leaf parsley, very finely chopped

1 bunch spring onions, finely chopped

2 garlic cloves, finely chopped

200ml (7fl oz) extra virgin olive oil

200g (7oz) thick Greek yoghurt

1 egg yolk

salt and pepper to taste

1 Soak the stale bread in water, then squeeze all the water out.

2 Put the soaked bread into a blender or food processor with the capers, and purée.

3 While the motor is running, add the parsley, spring onions and garlic. Pour in the olive oil bit by bit, then the yoghurt. Add the egg yolk and adjust the seasoning.

the tomatoes and
vineyards of santorini

You should always visit Santorini in the spring or autumn because only then can you watch the spectacle of life pouring out of the soil and into the plants. In the spring all is green and growing in the autumn there's the astonishing bounty of the harvest.

The first name of the island was "Strogili", given to it because of its round shape; later on it was named "Kallisti", which translates as "very beautiful", so as well as picking your season you should try to make the journey by ferry and not by plane. The overnight ferry will be pulling into harbour just as the sun rises, and your first dramatic view as you approach the island is to be savoured. As the island's earth is a mixture of dust and ashes, and easily dug, the land is incredibly fertile – something you take in at a glance on that first trip. When the ferry drops its anchor, all you will see is the black of the hills, the white of the houses, and the blue of the sea, with calm and sunshine overlaying everything.

Santorini is a newcomer to the Cyclades, arriving late courtesy of a volcanic eruption, so its history is more enigmatic than that of its neighbours. It is a history that must be rewritten every now and then. The hills, the sun, the sea, the sun-ripened tomatoes, the intertwined vines, and the glorious wines all play a role in the make-up of one of our most beautiful islands. I often catch myself daydreaming about Santorini. I picture myself sitting on a balcony entranced by the wonderful sunset, the traditional houses, the steady and remorseless pace of life. Everywhere I look there is a blue intensity that makes me wish for heavy curtains to shield the view and save it only for me.

This is the site of Akrotiri, one of the oldest civilizations in the Mediterranean, which flourished 4000 years ago, before all was covered by ash from the volcano. All the villages are far from the sea. Fira, one of the biggest towns, is at least half an hour away from where the ferry drops you. Last time I visited Santorini was after the Greek Easter, and I went with my business partner, Paloma, to taste the new wine vintages. In the early evening hours we wandered along the small streets soaking up memories to take home to London: vibrant memories of places, food smells and flavours, iced coffees, and new wines. It fascinates me that during my stays in Santorini I become another person – more expressive – and that when I leave the island those wonderful harvest dishes such as *dolmades*, tomato *keftedes* and *Fanouropita* (an olive oil cake named in honour of St Fanourios) can transport me straight back there again in the twinkling of an eye. This is partly because the lack of water and the effect of the island's volcanic soils make for distinctive local crops such as fava, white aubergines, small tomatoes, grapes, capers, prickly pears, and figs – all of which lend themselves to wonderful, intensely flavoured dishes.

pan-fried fava cakes

φαβοκεφτέδες τηγανητοί

*An increasing number of supermarkets have a section devoted to
Greek foods, and fava is likely to be there. But do not confuse fava with the fava bean, which is an
alternative name for the dried broad bean. There is the vexed question of whether to rinse the fava or
not. It is true that rinsing before cooking will save you time spent skimming later, but even
mentioning this strategy irritates my mother, who believes that if you are to experience the genuine
earthy flavours of fava you should never rinse. She says that rinsing fava "is like kissing someone and
then wiping your mouth".*

makes about 16 cakes

250g (9oz) *fava* (the best comes
   from Santorini) or, if pushed,
   yellow dhal

55g (2oz) shallots (or onions),
   finely diced

2 garlic cloves, finely diced

2 bay leaves

salt and pepper to taste

100ml (3½fl oz) extra virgin olive oil

1 tbsp fresh thyme leaves

finely grated zest of ½ lemon

To finish

200g (7oz) fine semolina

100g (3½oz) spring onions, finely
   chopped

½ bunch each of mint and
   parsley, chopped

finely grated zest of 2 lemons

groundnut oil for frying

1   First, cook the basic *fava* purée by covering the fava with water,
bringing to the boil, and then simmering for 35 minutes, or until the
fava is soft (decide for yourself whether to rinse it after reading the
introduction to this recipe). Then place it in a saucepan with the
shallots, garlic and bay leaves, and cover with cold water. Bring to the
boil and simmer for 50–60 minutes, until everything is soft and has
disintegrated to a purée.

2   Season with salt and pepper, and add a little boiling water. Mix in
the olive oil, thyme, and lemon zest. Let it sit uncovered for some
hours, until the *fava* soaks up all the water and oil. You are aiming for a
texture that is like stiff mashed potato.

3   To make the cakes, mix together the fava purée, half the semolina,
spring onions and herbs. Mix the remaining semolina with the lemon
zest for a coating.

4   Shape the mixture into patties about 5cm (2in) in diameter and up
to 2cm (¾in) thick. Coat each in the semolina and lemon zest mixture
and fry in hot groundnut oil until golden brown and crisp. Drain on
kitchen paper and serve with tomato and caper *giahni* (see page 69).

santorinian dolmades

ντολμάδες Σαντορίνης

Unlike many dolmades (see the recipe on page 82), these ones from Santorini are made with offal. The texture of the liver makes an interesting variation.

makes about 60 dolmades

150ml (5fl oz) olive oil

1kg (2¼lb) shallots, finely chopped

2 garlic cloves, finely chopped

500g (18oz) lamb's liver, finely minced (they would use kid's liver on Santorini)

salt and pepper to taste

200g (7oz) short-grain rice

2 bunches spring onions, finely sliced

1 bunch flat-leaf parsley, finely chopped

1 bunch mint, finely chopped

500g (18oz) preserved vine leaves

to cook and serve

1 lemon, thinly sliced

1 litre (1¾ pints) chicken stock or water

3 eggs

juice of 2 lemons

1   Heat 100ml (3½floz) of the olive oil in a large casserole over a medium heat. Brown the shallots and garlic, then add the minced liver. Stir well and season with salt and pepper.

2   Add the rice and spring onions and, stirring constantly, cook for about 5 minutes. Add some more seasoning and 250ml (9fl oz) of water. Cover and simmer until the water is absorbed. The rice should be softening, but not cooked completely. Add the herbs and some more black pepper. Set aside to cool.

3   Lay each large vine leaf on a flat surface, vein-side up. Trim away the stem (cut into the bottom of the leaf). Put 1 tbsp of the lamb mixture into the leaf. Form the mixture into a cylindrical shape. Fold the bottom (stem side) of the leaf up, fold in both sides, then roll the top over for a tight fit. Place in a suitable pot, packing them in snugly so they cannot unwrap, and never more than two layers deep.

4   Spread the lemon slices over the *dolmades* and place a plate over the top to keep them submerged. Cover with the chicken stock or water and remaining olive oil. Bring to the boil, then turn down to a simmer and cook, covered, for an hour.

5   Prepare an *avgolemono* sauce (see page 10), using the eggs and lemon juice, then pour it into the pot and swish it around. Let it all rest for 30 minutes. The sauce should be thick and served over the *dolmades*.

keftedakia

κεφτεδάκια

The flavours of keftedakia *go well with the warm salad of purslane and chickpeas on page 97.*

makes about 24 meatballs

4 slices white bread

10g (¼oz) cumin seeds

250g (9oz) lamb mince

100g (3½oz) pork mince

100g (3½oz) banana shallots, finely chopped

1 bunch spring onions, finely chopped

2 whole eggs

150g (5½oz) fine breadcrumbs

150g (5½oz) plain flour

salt and pepper to taste

500ml (18fl oz) groundnut oil

1   Discard the crusts and soak the bread in water.

2   Toss the cumin seeds in a hot frying pan, then grind them in a mortar.

3   Put the lamb and pork mince in a large mixing bowl. Squeeze the water from the bread and add the bread to the mince with the cumin seeds, shallots, spring onions and eggs. Mix well with your hands, then let the mixture rest in the refrigerator for at least an hour.

4   To make the meatballs, first shape about 1 tbsp of the mixture into a ball. Mix the breadcrumbs and flour together and season with salt and pepper. Roll the meatballs in this coating.

5   Heat some of the groundnut oil, but don't let it reach smoking point.

6   Pan-fry the meatballs in batches for 10–12 minutes per batch. Keep turning them until crisp and evenly browned. Discard the oil after each batch to avoid contaminating each new set of meatballs with the burnt debris of the last. Drain on kitchen paper and serve hot or warm.

lent

Often "doing without" particular ingredients is the spur a cook needs to create a new dish, and over centuries the constraints of Lent (when Orthodox Greeks must avoid cooking with any ingredient that contains blood) have left our cuisine with a treasury of simple but delicious vegetarian dishes. There's the bean dish *gigandes plaki*, several stunning salads including a warm salad of chickpeas and *purslane,* and an aubergine and walnut dip, and an almost luxurious leek pilaff.

gialangi

ντολμαδάκια γιαλαντζί

These little meatless dolmades are very delicately flavoured – the faint sweetness of sultanas and the crunch of pine nuts go superbly with the tang of lemon. This is a traditional dish for "Clean Monday", the first day of Lent.

makes about 60 dolmades

2 x 250g (9oz) packs preserved
   vine leaves (young ones are best
   – look for the Odysea brand)
1 lemon, finely sliced
juice of 2 lemons
50ml (2fl oz) extra virgin olive oil
55g (2oz) strained Greek yoghurt

filling

150ml (5fl oz) olive oil
150g (5½oz) shallots, finely
   chopped
200g (7oz) spring onions,
   including the green part, finely
   chopped
2 garlic cloves, very finely chopped
250g (9oz) short-grain rice
1 bunch flat-leaf parsley, finely
   chopped
1 bunch dill, finely chopped
100g (3½oz) sultanas (preferably
   from Corinth)
100g (3½oz) pine nuts
juice of 1 lemon
salt and pepper to taste

1   To make the filling, heat 75ml (2½fl oz) of the olive oil in a pan, add the shallots and spring onions, and cook until soft but not coloured. Add the garlic after about 5 minutes. Keep the contents of the pan moving while you add the rice, parsley, dill, sultanas, pine nuts, lemon juice, and finally the remaining olive oil. Season the mixture and remove from the heat.

2   If you're using young vine leaves you won't need to blanch them in boiling water to make them pliable. Just separate the good ones from the broken ones. Place a layer of the broken leaves in the bottom of a large, heavy-bottomed pot with a lid.

3   Lay each large vine leaf on a flat surface, vein-side up. Trim away the stem (cut into the bottom of the leaf). Put 1 tbsp of the filling mixture into the leaf, then form the mixture into a cylindrical shape. Fold the bottom (stem side) up. Fold in both sides. Roll the top over for a tight fit. Place in the pot. Pack them in snugly so they cannot unwrap, and never more than two layers deep. You should make about 60 *dolmades*. Spread the lemon slices over the top of the *dolmades*.

4   Put a plate over the *dolmades*. Cover with 1.5 litres (2¾ pints) of water and bring to the boil, then turn down to a simmer and cook, covered, for an hour. After the first 30 minutes of cooking, add the lemon juice.

5   If there is any liquid left after this cooking, do not throw it away, but let it cool down and add it to the extra virgin olive oil and the yoghurt to make a dressing. If there isn't any cooking liquid left, just sprinkle the olive oil on the top and eat the *dolmades* with the yoghurt.

puréed fava

φάβα

During Lent, fava is made into a simple purée (which provides the raw material for the pan-fried fava cakes on page 77). When you are making this dip, however, you make treat the fava slightly differently. My mother says that "fava without spring onions is like a wedding night without games", so leave them out at your peril!

serves 12 as mezedes

500g (18oz) *fava* (or yellow split
  peas)
3 shallots
2 bay leaves
150ml (5fl oz) extra virgin olive oil
salt and pepper to taste
1 large bunch spring onions,
  including the green part, finely
  chopped
1 heaped tbsp thyme leaves

1   Place the *fava* in a large saucepan with the shallots and bay leaves. Cover with about 3cm (1¼in) of water and bring to the boil. Reduce to a simmer and cook for about 35 minutes, or until very soft. Skim as necessary.

2   Drain the *fava* but keep the cooking water. Remove the bay leaves and shallots, then put the *fava* into a liquidizer with 100ml (3½fl oz) of the extra virgin olive oil (alternatively you could use the fine disc of a hand-mouli and finish off with a whisk).

3   Process until you have a very light, smooth, pale mixture, adding a little of the cooking water if it seems too stodgy. Taste and season with sea salt and freshly ground black pepper.

4   Add the spring onions and thyme leaves to the mixture.

5   Serve in a bowl and drizzle the remaining extra virgin olive oil on to the surface to prevent the dish from cracking like a dried-up river bed. Some people like to add a squeeze of fresh lemon juice. Eat with plenty of crusty bread.

borlotti beans

χάντρες

Although the word "vegetarian" doesn't exist in our vocabulary, Lent has a powerful influence, and during the summer months Greeks become vegetarian by default. When the earthy smell of simmering borlotti beans drifted through our holiday house, we all knew that the next smell was going to be from the grilled fish but without the chips! The exact quantities of green herbs used are a matter of taste: a handful of each if they come from the garden, or one of those supermarket packs of each will do fine.

serves 4 as an accompaniment

500g (18oz) fresh borlotti beans
   (you can substitute tinned beans
   providing you drain and
   rinse them – see method)
100ml (3 ½fl oz) olive oil
1kg (2 ¼lb) leeks, white part only,
   finely chopped
1 fennel bulb, including the
   feathery leaves, finely diced
2 celery sticks, finely diced
5 garlic cloves, finely chopped
1kg (2 ¼lb) tomatoes, skinned,
   seeded and finely chopped
a generous amount of herbs,
   including oregano, celery tops,
   parsley, and chervil, finely
   chopped
salt and pepper to taste

1   Pod the borlotti beans if you are using fresh.

2   Heat the olive oil in a shallow casserole or a deep frying pan, then add the leeks, fennel, celery, garlic, and tomatoes and sweat with the lid on over a low heat.

3   Add the oregano and fresh beans if you are using them, season, and stir well. Add 1.5 litres (2¾ pints) warm water and simmer uncovered for an hour. If you are using tinned beans, cut back the water to 750ml (26fl oz) and the cooking time to 30 minutes.

4   Preheat the oven to 190°C/375°F/gas mark 5.

5   Add the remaining herbs, stir well, and adjust the seasoning. Spread the beans out in a roasting dish and bake for about 1¼ hours, until a light crust forms on top but the borlotti beans are still tender and juicy.

6   Remove from the oven and place the dish on a rack to cool. The beans taste best when eaten at room temperature.

aubergine and walnut salad

μελιτζανοσαλάτα με καρύδια Αράχωβας

Some years ago, when I first started preparing a few Greek dishes for my business partner, Paloma Campbell, she complained about how confusing it was for her when I continually used the word "salad". It was quite difficult to convince her that we Greeks have a whole series of "flexible" words. One of the most useful is "salad". In a Greek kitchen, even a dish made from whipped tarama paste is called "taramasalata". As ripe and glossy aubergines are one of the joys of late summer, and as an outdoor barbecue is the best way to give this dish that char-grilled flavour, it's best to save this salad-that-isn't-a-salad for the summer months.

serves 8 as mezedes

1kg (2¼lb) aubergines
55g (2oz) shelled walnuts
1 large shallot, very finely
    chopped
1 bunch spring onions, very finely
    chopped
1 bunch coriander, finely chopped
2 garlic cloves, very finely chopped
4 tbsp extra virgin olive oil
4 tsp lemon juice
salt and pepper to taste

1 Cook the aubergines on the barbecue until the skin is burnt and the flesh is soft. Set them aside until they are cool enough to handle. Scoop out the flesh into a large bowl and discard the skin. If there are any aubergine juices left in the bowl, pass them through a sieve and add to the aubergine pulp. This liquid will give an extra hint of smokiness to the aubergine. (Alternatively, if you do not have an outdoor barbecue, slice the aubergines lengthways and approximately 1cm/½in thick. Use a skillet to cook them until they are very soft. You will get an almost identical result.)

2 Preheat your oven to 180°C/350°F/gas mark 4.

3 Toast the walnuts in the oven for about 10 minutes, then chop them roughly.

4 Mix the shallot, spring onions, coriander, garlic, olive oil and lemon juice together in a salad bowl. Add the aubergine, using a fork to break it up, then add the walnuts. Check and adjust the seasoning.

clean monday – the first day of lent

Mention Lent, and I always think of my Uncle Theodore. He was a colonel in the Greek army and he was passionate about the mountains of western Macedonia. Uncle Theodore was a naturalist, and he enjoyed shooting, so for him one of the charms of the area was the profusion of game. Scattered through these wild mountains are a number of refuges, in which visitors can shelter from bad weather, and the last time I went walking there with my uncle we stayed in one on the night before "Clean Monday", when Lent begins. So that night we baked the traditional Lenten *lagana*, a simple bread that forms the perfect backdrop to all those assertive Lenten flavours.

In Greece, the guiding principle of the Lenten fast is that you should not eat anything that contains blood – so taramasalata, the first fresh garlic of the season, pickled vegetables, cannellini bean salad, olives, pickled octopus, octopus stew seasoned with cinnamon and orange peel, and served with *kritharaki* (tiny pasta the size and shape of pine needles), mussel pilaff, *spanakorizo* (spinach and leek pilaff with a generous drizzle of lemon juice), cuttlefish casserole, and endless bottles of wine from the newly opened vintage are all OK! I remember discussing with Uncle Theodore how ironic it is that all these amazing dishes – some of the best fare in Greek cooking – were born out of a need to be abstemious. If this is "spiritual and physical cleansing", we should all do more of it.

My uncle was a great believer in the "oxygenating walk", and in the early hours of the next morning we set off for a hike along the twisty footpaths of western Macedonia. As we left, an old lady sliced some home-made halva for us to eat during the day. Lent had begun. Halva is the most popular Lenten sweet, often made with sesame and sometimes mixed with nuts or chocolate – once again something that doesn't feel like self-denial.

You always feel good in the mountains. Western Macedonia is one of the most unspoiled parts of the Greek mainland, and the mountains run all the way up to the Albanian border. As far as we Greeks are concerned, the Alps begin near Epirus. These mountain days were a major source of inspiration when I was working on recipes for the Real Greek restaurant.

One of my favourite walks with my parents was on the steep slopes of the Pindos Mountains. I remember my father saying that if he had the chance to re-educate himself he would want to do it in the vineyard of "the humble saint", the martyr Nicholas of Metsovo, who was burnt alive by the Turks in 1617, upon refusing to betray his religious faith.

As a child I visited the town of Metsovo several times with my father, on trips to buy cheese for his delicatessen. An enduring local myth is that the herd there was started after World War II with stock from the herd of the young Queen Elizabeth II of England. The locals gave each of them a suitably "royal" name, and ordered wooden signs from a local workshop to go over each stall in the barn. To this day you can see the names written in large capital letters over each stall: Victoria, Mary, Elizabeth, and so forth.

The cheese factory of Metsovo became famous for combining the methods favoured by Italian cheese makers with the traditional Greek approach, although they continued to make the hard cheeses popular in the region. *Metsovone* cheese is just one of the local cheeses which has an Italian equivalent – it's called *provolone*. But Greeks will always argue that even Italians admit that *Metsovone* cheese is superior to *provolone*!

gigandes plaki

γίγαντες πλακί

This is one of the great classic dishes, but it suffers terribly if you substitute smaller beans for the huge, traditional gigandes. *The best* gigandes *come from Prespes and they resemble butter beans, although they have a more rounded appearance.*

serves 6 as an accompaniment

500g (18oz) *gigandes* beans
80–100ml (2½–3½fl oz) olive oil
2 red onions, roughly chopped
3 garlic cloves, roughly chopped
150g (5½oz) fresh plum
   tomatoes, skinned, seeded
   and roughly chopped
100g carrots, diced
2 celery sticks, including any
   leaves, roughly chopped
2 bay leaves
1 tbsp thyme leaves
salt and pepper to taste
2 tbsp chopped flat-leaf parsley

1   Wash the beans, then soak overnight in cold water.

2   The next day bring the beans to the boil, then discard the soaking water. Cover the beans again in fresh water, put the lid on, boil for 10 minutes, then simmer until they are just tender – a further 35–50 minutes, depending on how old the beans are.

3   Preheat the oven to 160°C/325°F/gas mark 3.

4   Heat the oil in a saucepan and sauté the onions and garlic until soft. Add the plum tomatoes, carrots, celery and celery leaves, and cook for about 10 minutes. Use a hand blender to purée the vegetables.

5   Put the vegetable mixture and the beans into a flat dish (this will help ensure they cook evenly) and stir together. Add the bay and the thyme leaves and season to taste with salt and pepper. Cook in the oven for 1½–2 hours, or until the beans are tender and almost all the liquid has been absorbed. Look at the dish occasionally and, if more liquid is needed, add a little hot water from a kettle. On no account add cold water as it will make the bean skins tough. Leave to cool with the lid on, and the beans will go on swelling.

6   Add the parsley and stir well before serving. Eat the *gigandes* at room temperature, rather than refrigerator-cold.

macedonian aubergines

μελιτζάνες τουρσί από την μακεδονία

If the weather is cool, you can leave the pickle outside the refrigerator to mature, but either way you should let the flavours infuse for a couple of days before eating.

serves 6

1kg (2¼lb) aubergines (small ones – this pickle is only worth making when they are in season)

a few celery leaves

1 bunch spring onions, finely sliced

125ml (4fl oz) extra virgin olive oil

2 garlic cloves, very finely chopped

25ml (1fl oz) lemon juice

salt and pepper to taste

1 Fill your largest pot half-full with water and bring to the boil. Add the aubergines. Boil for approximately 10 minutes, or until they feel quite soft when you stab them with a knife. Remember to turn them over a couple of times with a wooden spoon while cooking, as they need to be cooked evenly.

2 Remove the aubergines with a straining spoon. Hang them from the washing line and let any water they absorbed during cooking drain away.

3 Blanch the celery leaves and spring onions for 4–5 minutes in a smaller pot of boiling water. Drain.

4 When the aubergines are well drained, chop them coarsely. Place them in a large bowl with the blanched celery leaves and spring onions, the olive oil, garlic, lemon juice, and seasoning, and mix well.

beetroot salad

παντζαροσαλάτα

This simple Lenten dish uses both the beetroots themselves and the leafy green tops that are so often thrown away – Greek cooks are perfectly in tune with the idea of waste not, want not! If you cannot find fresh leafy beets, make the dish anyway, as the rich flavours are a joy.

serves 8

2kg (4½lb) good, firm, fresh beetroot (if including the leaves, otherwise 1kg/2¼lb)

salt and pepper to taste

20 Santorinian pickled caper leaves (or 25g/1oz capers)

100ml (3½fl oz) extra virgin olive oil

2 tbsp aged Corinthian red wine vinegar

1   Cut off and reserve the beetroot tops and roots. Wash the beetroot without removing the skins, then cook them in a large pot with plenty of salted water.

2   Clean the beetroot leaves with the stems. Add them to the pot when the beetroot have been cooking for 30 minutes. When the beetroot are tender (which will depend on their size), remove and strain off the liquid.

3   Peel the beetroot and cut them into wedges. Chop up the greens. Add the caper leaves and mix well. Pour the olive oil and vinegar over the top and adjust the seasoning.

leek pilaff

προσόρυζο

At Rovies, the agricultural cooperative on the island of Evoia, the kitchen is the domain of Koula, and she is one of the most impulsive cooks I have ever come across. Koula comes from western Macedonia and has a natural ability to put several dishes together seemingly without thinking much about it. The last time my friend Panagiotis and I visited Rovies, she served this outstanding simple pilaff with lakerda *(preserved fillets of torik, which is similar to tuna). If you can't find* lakerda, *use pickled herring, smoked mackerel, or some other salty, strong-tasting preserved fish instead. Another delicious option is to stir in some sea-urchin roe – then the dish is properly called "prassorizo".*

serves 4

100ml (3½fl oz) olive oil
1kg (2¼lb) leeks, trimmed, washed well, and finely chopped
55g (2oz) tomato *perasti* (the Greek equivalent of tomato passata)
1 bunch dill, finely chopped
½ bunch mint, finely chopped
250g (9oz) short-grain rice
salt and pepper to taste
1 lemon, thinly sliced
100g (3½oz) butter

1   Heat the olive oil in a pan, add the leeks and soften them over a low heat, stirring with a wooden spoon.

2   Add the tomato *perasti*, dill, mint, and enough water to half cover the leek – about 250ml (9fl oz). Stir in the rice and some salt and pepper to taste. Arrange the lemon slices over the surface of the rice and cook, still over a low heat, with the lid on, until all the liquid has been absorbed by the ingredients – about 25 minutes. The rice should be ready when it is tender and the surface has "many holes".

3   Remove the lemon slices and discard. Slice the butter thinly and arrange the slices over the surface, put the lid back on, and let the rice rest for 10–15 minutes without stirring before serving.

warm salad of chickpeas with purslane

ρεβιθοσαλάτα με γλιστρίδα

When it comes to cooking chickpeas, I always remember my mother saying, "As you look at the chickpeas in the pot they look back at you, like characters that have stepped out from the memory shadows where they have been hiding away." Perhaps each chickpea does have its own passions and obsessions... they certainly go well with purslane.

serves 8

250g (9oz) chickpeas, soaked overnight, drained and rinsed

300g (10½oz) button onions

100g (3½oz) bacon in 1 piece, rind removed

750ml (26fl oz) chicken stock

500g (18oz) *purslane* (or watercress)

125ml (4fl oz) olive oil

salt and pepper to taste

1 Put everything except the *purslane*, olive oil, and seasoning into a large pot with 500ml (18fl oz) of water, put the lid on, and bring to the boil. Boil for 10 minutes, then turn down the heat and simmer for a further 50 minutes.

2 Pick over the purslane leaves and chop any very thick stems finely. Add to the pot and continue simmering for another 30 minutes.

3 Add the olive oil and simmer for 10–15 minutes more. Remove from the heat, season, and let the dish cool down. Discard the bacon.

4 This salad should be eaten at room temperature as an accompaniment to boiled eggs, fried meatballs, or even leftover meats.

"...all these amazing Lenten dishes – some of the best fare in Greek cooking – were born out of a need to be abstemious."

octopus with red wine vinegar

χταποδάκι με κρασόξιδο

The key to cooking octopus is to understand its texture. Octopuses are mainly composed of water. In Greece they can be hung out to dry in the sun, but cooks elsewhere must find a way to drive off the water and concentrate the taste.

serves 4

1 x 1kg (2¼lb) whole octopus

2 garlic cloves

125ml (4fl oz) extra virgin olive oil

2 tbsp aged Corinthian red wine vinegar

1 bunch thyme, leaves only

1   Place a large, heavy-bottomed pot on the heat and let it get very hot. Put the octopus into it and pop the lid on. Turn the heat down to the minimum and cook for 40–50 minutes, until the octopus is tender (test by cutting the thickest part of the leg).

2   Remove the octopus and let it cool down. In the meantime reduce the pot juices to approximately 100ml (3½fl oz). Keep an eye on things because the liquid will be quite sticky and it will burn very quickly.

3   Put the garlic into a liquidizer and blitz, then start adding the oil a little at a time. Finally add the vinegar and the reduced juices. You should end up with a well-mixed dressing.

4   Cut off the legs of the octopus and leave them whole. Remove the beak with a paring knife and cut the head into quarters.

5   Place the octopus pieces in a large mixing bowl, pour the dressing on the top, sprinkle with the thyme leaves, and mix well. It is best to leave this dish covered in the refrigerator for a day before eating, so that the flavours deepen.

easter lamb

Greeks eat fish, game, pork, and beef – much the same as everybody else – but we save a special place in our affections for lamb. Lamb is always at the centre of any Easter celebrations. Here are the recipes for simply roasting a shoulder of lamb to serve with oregano potatoes and, for more ambitious cooks, the marinade and techniques for roasting a whole lamb. Also here are the recipe and directions for making the ultimate *souvlaki*.

easter lamb and oregano potatoes

αρνάκι στον φούρνο με πατάτες ριγανάτες

In Greece each family has an Easter lamb, and choosing the perfect animal is a business of much the same magnitude as selecting the Christmas turkey in Britain. If a whole lamb seems daunting, make the dish with a shoulder of lamb and start by marinating it overnight. The shoulder works better than other joints as the fat helps keep the meat juicy during its cooking, so do not trim away all that fat!

shoulder of lamb

serves 4

1 shoulder of lamb
salt and pepper to taste
50ml (2fl oz) olive oil

overnight marinade
4 garlic cloves, finely chopped
½ bunch each of oregano, thyme,
  and rosemary, chopped
100ml (3½fl oz) olive oil
100ml (3½fl oz) lemon juice
200ml (7fl oz) red wine

lamb dry rub
4 garlic cloves
¼ bunch each of oregano, thyme,
  and rosemary

potatoes
1kg (2¼lb) roasting potatoes
4 tsp lemon juice
finely grated zest of 1 lemon
50ml (2fl oz) olive oil
½ bunch oregano

1 Combine all the marinade ingredients and season to taste. Place the lamb shoulder in a large, deep container and pour in the marinade. Turn the lamb in the marinade so that it is coated all over. Cover and refrigerate overnight. When you take the lamb out, set the marinade to one side.

2 Using a pestle and mortar, crush the ingredients for the dry rub together until they form a paste. Season to taste.

3 Make 10–15 small incisions all over the surface of the marinated shoulder using a small, sharp paring knife. Stuff each of these little holes with the dry rub and rub whatever is left over the surface of the lamb. Season well with salt and pepper and rub the lamb with the olive oil.

4 Preheat the oven to 220°C/425°F/gas mark 7. Cut the potatoes into wedges lengthways. Place them in a large roasting pan and toss with the lemon juice, zest, olive oil, and oregano. Season well with salt and pepper. Place the lamb on a rack over the potatoes, and put in the oven.

5 After the first 20 minutes, turn the oven down to 180°C/350°F/gas mark 4. Roast, basting the lamb and potatoes often with the pan juices, for a further 1¼ hours, depending on the weight, or until the lamb is cooked through. If necessary, add some marinade during roasting to stop everything drying out. Remove the lamb from the oven and let it rest for about 20 minutes before carving. Turn the oven off and leave the potatoes in it to keep warm until you are ready to serve.

whole spring lamb

serves 10

1 whole spring lamb, 6–7kg
(13–15¼lb) in weight
salt and pepper to taste

lamb dry rub
6–8 garlic cloves
2 tbsp each of dried oregano,
thyme, and rosemary leaves

lamb "wash"
juice of 3 lemons
75ml (2½fl oz) olive oil

potatoes
3kg (6½lb) roasting potatoes, cut
lengthways into wedges
finely grated zest of 2 lemons
50ml (2fl oz) lemon juice
½ bunch oregano, finely chopped
1 bunch flat-leaf parsley, finely
chopped

1 Preheat the oven to 220°C/425°F/gas mark 7.

2 Using a pestle and mortar, crush all the ingredients for the dry rub together until they form a paste.

3 Wash the lamb with the lemon juice, inside and out, then rub it with half the olive oil.

4 Make 10–15 small incisions all over the surface of the lamb using a small, sharp paring knife. Stuff each of these little holes with the dry rub, and rub whatever is left over the surface of the lamb. Season well with salt and pepper and rub the lamb with the remaining olive oil.

5 With a needle and butcher's string, close the belly of the lamb and plug the rear with a wad of wet cotton wool. This is important as it keeps the steam inside.

6 Place the lamb on a rack and put it in the oven. After the first 20 minutes, turn the oven down to 180°C/350°F/gas mark 4. Keep basting frequently. About 2½ hours later, lift the roasting rack and add the potatoes. Continue to roast for about 1¼ hours, basting both the lamb and the potatoes with the pan juices. Remove the lamb and let it rest for 30 minutes before carving.

7 Meanwhile add the lemon zest and juice to the potatoes and return them to the oven for a further 20 minutes to get some colour. Remove from the oven and sprinkle them with the chopped oregano and parsley.

"As the generations replace one another, they do so to a backdrop of roasting lamb."

the sizzle on the spit

It is mid February or maybe the beginning of March, and we're walking down the streets of Naxos, one of the Aegean islands, to meet my father's friend, a local shepherd, and fetch a lamb for Easter. We make this trip every year, and every year I feel that it is full of hidden possibilities. Each year I feel a little closer to something momentous – enlightenment, if you will. Maybe it is the beauty of the islands, or the simple timeless rituals of the shepherd. Even as we set out from my parents' house in Halandri I sense something special, but it is always tantalizingly out of reach. I struggle to get a handle on my feelings, and although I can see a beginning and an end the joyful gap between the two eludes me. As I have grown older I have realized that in itself waiting to understand is no bad thing, especially when the waiting is the patient, observant waiting of a shepherd – the shepherd is probably the only person for whom infinity begins at the end of his own thumb.

The smell and flavour of roast lamb stimulate my senses in many ways. They can be a link to the past, calling up memories of the older generations of the family, or they can be a bridge to the future, symbolizing our own transition from youngsters to mature people. As the generations replace one another, they do so to a backdrop of roasting lamb.

The lamb is centre stage in a story that has been woven from the same plot for many years: Easter gatherings in my parents' garden, standing around the spits with the slowly turning lambs and *kokoretsi* (the entrails cooked on a spit). The lamb means "Easter" because Christians view Jesus Christ as "the lamb of God" – sent as a sacrifice for the sins of the world. Also, Christian believers refer to the Lord as "the good shepherd" who watches over them. Jesus also was seen as the sacrificial lamb. This lamb, known as the Pascal lamb, was borrowed from the Jewish feast of the Passover, also a spring feast.

But my father had a different slant on the philosophical elements of the Easter festivities. He preferred to see Easter as the festival of spring, the vernal equinox, and he saw it as a resurrection for nature after the long, dark months of winter. So it was inevitable that Easter would be a feast of liberation and promise. And as the celebration days were approaching, the sacrifice of the lamb was essential. I suppose that a rabbit could have taken the place of the lamb on the spit, but rabbits are notable for their endless capacity for reproduction, rather than as a symbol of rebirth (which is perhaps why some clever entrepreneur turned them into chocolate bunnies, and so made a lot of money out of Easter).

I still remember with pleasure some of the theological debates that rolled around the Easter table, but I personally enjoy our Greek legends more. In the Greek myths, this is the time of year when the goddesses, Demeter and Persephone, return from the underworld bringing with them the light of day.

It seems that, however you view it, in the end history is a circle, and to remind us of that we have the flavoursome lamb turning and sizzling on a spit with the aromatic smell of mountain oregano.

the real greek souvlaki and its trimmings

το γνήσιο ελληνικό σουβλάκι

I was brought up to believe that souvlaki *should be a seasonal dish, made with pork between late autumn and Easter, then made with lamb for the rest of the year. As you never eat one* souvlaki, *but always several, do not overload them – make them petite. For us Greeks the souvlaki is as important as the pizza is for Italians, a key part of our street food. There are two things worth noting if you want the perfect souvlaki: the meat should come from a young animal (you can use either the leg or the shoulder), and it should be served with genuine flat breads and not the pitta pockets that are so common in Britain.*

makes 10 souvlaki

1kg (2¼lb) shoulder of lamb (or
   lean pork)
1 bunch thyme, chopped
4 garlic cloves, crushed
finely grated zest and juice of
   2 lemons
300ml (10fl oz) olive oil
100ml (3½fl oz) red wine
salt and pepper to taste

to serve

10 Greek flat breads
1 quantity *tzatziki* (see page 165)
   at room temperature
250g (9oz) ripe tomatoes, sliced
2 pickled cucumbers, sliced
   lengthways
sweet paprika, as much as your
   palate can take

1   Trim any excess fat off the meat. Cut the meat into walnut-sized pieces. Place it in a bowl and add the thyme, garlic, lemon zest, 100ml (3½fl oz) of the olive oil, red wine and seasoning. Mix well and wrap the meat and flavourings tightly in clingfilm. Refrigerate, ideally overnight, for the meat to absorb all the flavours.

2   About half an hour before grilling, drain off the meat marinade juices and reserve. Preheat the barbecue or grill. In a small jar with a lid, combine the marinade juices with the lemon juice and remaining olive oil. Screw the lid on and shake until the dressing is amalgamated.

3   Thread the chunks of meat on to long skewers and brush with some of the dressing. Over hot coals, barbecue the *souvlaki* until they are done the way you like them. Remove the skewers from the barbecue and rest the meat in a bowl for 10 minutes. In the bottom of the bowl should be some delicious meat juices.

4   Brush the flat breads with the dressing, then dip them in the meat juices. Throw them on the hot barbecue and let them get some colour, but do not allow them to become crisp.

5   Arrange the meat on the flat bread, spread on some *tzatziki* and top with sliced tomatoes, pickled cucumber, and a sprinkle of sweet paprika. Roll the flat bread in a piece of parchment paper and serve.

tsoureki

πασχαλινό τσουρέκι

In the Greek Orthodox calendar, Easter represents one of the busiest days of the year in the kitchen. My mother was always absorbed by her continuing search for culinary perfection. This is a traditional Greek Easter bread. Mahlepi is a Middle Eastern spice with no perfect equivalent; mastic is a resin used as flavouring all over Greece, but once again there is no ready equivalent – both are available in Middle Eastern shops.

makes 2 plaited loaves

10g (¼oz) star anise

100g (3½oz) caster sugar

150g (5½oz) butter

6 eggs

250ml (9fl oz) lukewarm milk

25g (1oz) fresh yeast

1 tbsp *mahlepi*

3 pieces mastic, crushed with a
  touch of sugar

1kg (2¼lb) strong white bread flour

olive oil for brushing

2 eggs, beaten with a little milk,
  for egg wash

150g (5½oz) split almonds

2 hard-boiled eggs, dyed red (use
  red onion skins for the dye)

1   Put 300ml (10fl oz) of water and the star anise into a pan, bring to the boil, and reduce to 75ml (2½fl oz) of anise infusion. Let it cool down.

2   Preheat the oven to 80°C/175°F/the lowest gas you can.

3   In a large mixing bowl, beat the sugar and butter to a light cream. Add the eggs one at a time. Slowly add the lukewarm milk, yeast, *mahlepi*, and mastic, and mix well. Start adding the flour gradually, and mix until everything is combined and the dough looks soft. Add the star anise infusion. Keep kneading the dough until it is very smooth. This will take 20 minutes by hand or 10 minutes in the mixer.

4   Place the *tsoureki* dough in a large container that will fit in your oven and that has enough room to let the dough expand. Brush the top with olive oil, then cover it with a damp cloth and a couple of clean kitchen cloths to retain the warmth. Put it in the oven to rise for approximately 1½ hours.

5   Punch the dough down and divide it into six pieces. Roll each part into a long baguette, pulling to stretch further. Join three of these together and braid as if plaiting a pigtail. Do the same with the remaining three pieces. Place the loaves on well-oiled baking sheets. Brush the *tsoureki* with the egg wash. Press the almonds into the surface and lodge one of the red eggs in the centre, between the braiding, of each loaf.

6 Set aside in a warm place to rise once more for about an hour.

7 Turn the temperature of the oven up to 200°C/400°F/gas mark 6. When the *tsoureki* loaves have risen enough, bake for 15 minutes. Turn the heat down to 180°C/350°F/gas mark 4 and bake for a further 25–30 minutes, or until the loaves look slightly brown. They should sound hollow when tapped. Place on a cooling rack to cool down.

island life

The isolated nature of island living has helped to create a special kind of cuisine. When a trip to the shops means a major expedition (and one that is often only possible when the sea is calm), cooking becomes simpler and more self-reliant. Dishes such as Cretan *dakos* (a kind of super bruschetta made with prawns), roast feta with oregano, rolled fresh sardines, pan-fried olives, or watermelon and feta salad are gloriously intense.

rolled fresh sardines

σαρδέλες τυλιχτές

The flash of bright silver from fresh sardines draws your eye. These fish are so insubstantial and yet so very tasty!

serves 6–8

1 bunch flat-leaf parsley, finely
    chopped
200g (7oz) rusks, or old bread,
    turned into fine breadcrumbs
1 tsp ground cumin
finely grated zest of 1 lemon
150g (5½oz) Santorinian capers
freshly ground black pepper
1kg (2¼lb) sardines (ask your
    fishmonger to "butterfly" and
    bone them)
500ml (18fl oz) olive oil
100ml (3½fl oz) lemon juice
500g (18oz) ripe tomatoes, cut
    into wedges

1 In a large bowl, mix the parsley, breadcrumbs, cumin, lemon zest, capers, and black pepper to taste.

2 Lay the prepared sardines flat on the chopping board, skin side down. Spread the mixture evenly on to the fish and roll them firmly from the tail to the head so that the thick end of the fish protects the thin end during cooking. Arrange them in a saucepan – they should be tightly packed. Pour over the olive oil and lemon juice, and cook, uncovered, over a low heat for about 20 minutes.

3 Remove from the heat and allow to cool. Add the tomato wedges and eat cold.

watermelon and feta salad

καρπούζι με φέτα

A fresh but intensely flavoured salad with the contrasting flavours and textures of watermelon and roast feta.

serves 6

100ml (3½fl oz) extra virgin olive oil
juice and finely grated zest of
  1 lemon
1 bunch spring onions, finely sliced
salt and pepper to taste
250g (9oz) feta, in big pieces
1 tbsp soft brown sugar
1 medium watermelon, seeded
  and cut into large chunks
½ bunch mint, leaves only (keep
  in iced water until needed)

1   Preheat the oven to 200°C/400°F/gas mark 6.

2   Put 75ml (2½fl oz) of the extra virgin olive oil, the lemon juice, spring onions and seasoning in a jar with a lid and shake well until all the ingredients are well amalgamated.

3   Place the feta pieces on a roasting tray and sprinkle with the sugar, lemon zest, and remaining olive oil. Add a twist of pepper and roast for 10 minutes.

4   Place the watermelon in a large salad bowl and add the roast feta and its juices, plus the dressing with the spring onions. Mix well, then finally sprinkle with the well-drained mint leaves.

kayganas with akrokolion

καγιανάς με ακροκώλιον Ευρυτανίας

This is a kind of superior ham omelette. Take a bottle of ouzo out of the cupboard with some olives, pickled green chilli peppers and mature goaty Greek cheeses, and eat and drink with your friends. This dish is perfect for when you come to a break in the conversation.

serves 4

egg mix

5 eggs
1 tbsp strong plain flour
50ml (2fl oz) ouzo

filling

1 tbsp olive oil and a knob of
  butter for frying
1 spring onion, including the
  green part, very finely sliced
salt and coarsely ground black
  pepper to taste
200g (7oz) *akrokolion* (a
  wonderful Greek dried ham),
  or prosciutto, very thinly sliced
sweet paprika to taste
2 tbsp thyme honey

1 Whisk all the egg mix ingredients together with 2 tbsp of water and keep in the refrigerator, covered, until ready to cook.

2 For the filling, melt the olive oil and butter together in a large frying pan over a medium heat. When they start to sizzle, add the sliced spring onion and, 1 minute later, the egg mixture. Lower the heat and season with salt and coarsely ground black pepper.

3 Cover the egg surface with the *akrokolion* (or prosciutto) and fold the "omelette" in half. Turn over and cook for a couple of extra minutes; it is ready when the centre is still just about runny.

4 Sprinkle with the paprika and finally a drizzle of honey, which works amazingly well as a contrast to the salty ham.

roast feta with oregano

φέτα στο φούρνο με βουνίσιο θυμάρι

Cheese is one of the fundamental ingredients of Greek mezedes. And this is a deliciously simple way of presenting roast cheese.

serves 6

500g (18oz) feta, preferably
  barrel-aged
200ml (7fl oz) olive oil
2 tbsp dried oregano
coarsely ground black pepper
1 lemon, washed and cut into
  6 wedges

1 Preheat the oven to 200°C/400°F/gas mark 6.

2 Cut six 15cm (6in) squares each of kitchen foil and baking parchment. Place the foil sheets on a roasting tray and lay the parchment papers on top.

3 Cut the feta into six 2cm (¾in) thick pieces and place them on the pre-cut parchment paper and foil. Drizzle with the olive oil, sprinkle with the dried oregano, and add pepper to taste and a lemon wedge. Fold them into six parcels.

4 Bake for 15 minutes. Open the parcels at the table and squeeze the hot lemon over the cheese.

the island of love

The myth of an island of love is an old one and crops up in the literature of both France and Italy. As you would expect, the island in question is to be found in Greece, and its name is Kythera – the birthplace of Aphrodite.

An island is a great place to develop a cuisine. Cooks are invariably forced to work with what to the mainlander might seem like a restricted palette, and island cuisine is bound to be seasonal. Great ingenuity is needed to rework the same ingredients and themes time and time again while keeping them fresh. Island people are often on the breadline, so there is little extravagance. And whatever you have is what you cook with – there is no dashing to a corner shop for some lemongrass or water chestnuts. Island food has an honesty about it that is always appealing.

One of my favourite romantic paintings is by Watteau – *L'Embarquement pour l'Ile de Kythère* – and the voyage to Kythera, the island of love, has become a metaphor that to Greeks has much of the feel of the proverb "It is better to travel hopefully than to arrive". Any voyage to "Kythera" is a difficult undertaking, and it is a journey that many pilgrims set out on, but never complete, allowing the island to stay alluring and elusive, a land of eternal destination, an impossible dream and an ideal beauty.

I most recently visited Kythera on the sailing yacht "Larne". We had mentally prepared ourselves for a long and difficult crossing from Mani, but the sea and the wind were so friendly that the journey was an anti-climax. And in the perfect weather of the approaching autumn we arrived on the island of love. The locals were all busy watching the behaviour of the migrating songbirds. The birds had arrived a week earlier than usual, and so the Kytherians were preparing themselves for an especially hard winter. The island is an important staging post for the birds as they get ready to fly to North Africa. Equally, during antiquity Kythera was an important staging post for anyone sailing between Greece, Egypt, Syria, Libya and Tunisia. And because of this strategic importance, Kythera was squabbled over by the two regional powers, Sparta and Athens.

We spent the first night in the main town of Kythera, where we had some of the best food I have ever tasted in my frequent trips home to Greece. As the sun broke through the mist, it dissolved and the sky cleared over Kythera. Although it was tempting to set sail and leave with the fine weather, we could hear the chugging of the first fishing boat returning to the sheltered harbour. Fresh anchovies were the main catch, so we rolled some money into an empty film case and deputized one of our party to swim out and intercept the fisherman before he reached the dock. After two weeks of sailing we had collected plenty of sea salt from the deck of the boat. We used it to cure the anchovies with some good, local red wine vinegar and plenty of sliced garlic. After putting the fish aside to marinate, the difficult part was waiting until dinner time to taste them. That's what I love about eating back at home: we eat first with our imagination and the anticipation is all.

That evening, we watched the sun set over the meeting place of three seas – the Aegean, Ionian and Cretan – painting all with scarlet reflections. Alexandros, captain of the "Larne" and a perfect storyteller, said that as legend tells it, during a skirmish among the gods, a piece of the never-ending Sky fell (due to an aggressive slash from Cronos) into the life-giving Sea, who wrapped it with her froth, and thus Aphrodite was born. He continued that it was at Kythera that Zephyros rendered Aphrodite up to the world and prepared her to take her place on the mythological mountain of Olympus. He finished his tale with the first sentence of a Greek poem:

"That we've broken their statues,
That we've driven them out of their temples,
Doesn't mean at all that the gods are dead."

At that moment I became aware of how far I was from my life in London. We were lying in a heavenly haze off the island of love, eating fresh anchovies, fully ripened figs that we had collected from the numerous trees on the island, and a savoury ewe's milk cheese from Crete – every taste intense and perfect.

cretan dakos with prawns

κρητικός ντάκος με γαρίδες

"Dakos" is the Cretan equivalent of Italy's bruschetta or the Catalan tapa of toasted bread rubbed with oil and tomato. The addition of prawns turns a simple appetizer into something special.

makes 8 dakos

150ml (5fl oz) olive oil

3 garlic cloves, halved

½ bunch oregano, finely chopped

500g (18oz) large uncooked
    prawns, shelled but heads on

1kg (2¼lb) ripe tomatoes

100g (3½oz) caper leaves

100ml (3½fl oz) extra virgin olive oil

salt and pepper to taste

8 toasts (made by slow baking 8
    thick slices French bread until crisp)

200g (7oz) St Michael cheese (a
    very hard cow's milk cheese
    from the island of Syros) or
    Parmesan, grated

1 Put the olive oil, garlic, and oregano in a saucepan and place over a low heat with the lid on for about 30 minutes to infuse the oil. It is important to keep the oil at a very low temperature.

2 Add the prawns and cook on the same low heat for about 15 minutes more, until the prawns are cooked through. Remove the saucepan from the heat and let everything cool down for 5 minutes. Remove the prawns from the oil and reserve both.

3 Meanwhile, skin the tomatoes by putting them in just boiled water for a few seconds, then lifting them out and allowing them to cool before removing the skin. Seed them and chop the flesh. Put them in a colander and let them drain for 20 minutes. You will need the tomato juices, so place a bowl underneath.

4 Put the tomatoes, caper leaves, and extra virgin olive oil into a large mixing bowl. Chop the prawns and add them to the tomato mixture. Season well.

5 Dip the toasts in the tomato juices for a few seconds to soften them. Place each toast on a small plate, spread with some of the softened garlic, and drizzle with the infused olive oil.

6 Spoon the tomato and prawn mixture equally over the toasts. Sprinkle with the grated St Michael cheese, salt, and pepper, and drizzle with the remaining infused olive oil. Let them sit for a few minutes before you eat them.

purslane, yoghurt and walnut salad

σαλάτα με γλιστρίδα, γιαούρτι και καρύδια

Purslane is an under-rated leaf. For some reason, it has fallen out of favour and may be hard to obtain. If you can't find any, substitute watercress, which is just as robust.

serves 4

250g (9oz) *purslane* (or watercress)
100ml (3½fl oz) extra virgin olive oil
2 garlic cloves, very finely chopped
juice of 1 lemon
200g (7oz) thick Greek yoghurt
75g (2¾oz) shelled walnuts,
   crushed in a pestle and mortar
salt and pepper to taste

1   Pick over the *purslane* leaves and remove any very thick stems. Wash the leaves well.

2   Put the olive oil, garlic, and lemon juice into a blender or food processor, and turn the motor to the fastest speed. Let the motor run for a few minutes, until you have a good, cloudy sauce. Slow down the motor and add the yoghurt a little at a time. Mix well and remove the bowl from the machine.

3   With a plastic spoon, fold in the crushed walnuts and then adjust the seasoning.

4   Dress the *purslane* leaves with the mixture and refrigerate the salad until it is needed.

"...back at home, we eat first with our imagination and the anticipation is all."

spinach and yoghurt salad

σαλάτα με σπανάκι και γιαούρτι

My parents firmly believed that certain flavours were not for every day and that having something all the time diminished its appeal. A perfect example is mayonnaise. As kids we were obsessed with its flavour and texture. We wanted to dip everything into it. My father was keen that we enjoy our own national delicacies and convinced us that spinach and yoghurt salad was every bit as good as mayonnaise. So this is what we took to dip our boiled potatoes into when we went out fishing. When we were a bit older and wiser – teenagers hanging around the house – we substituted chips for the boiled potatoes. What a flavour!

serves 6

1kg (2¼lb) spinach, washed and
   finely shredded
1 bunch mint, finely chopped
3 spring onions, including the
   green part, finely chopped
2 garlic cloves, crushed
400g (14oz) strained Greek
   yoghurt
2 tbsp extra virgin olive oil
salt and pepper to taste
55g (2oz) butter

1   Mix together the spinach, mint, spring onions, garlic, yoghurt, and olive oil. Season to taste.

2   Melt the butter, taking care that it does not burn, and pour it over the salad.

runner bean salad

αμπελοφάσουλα με λαδολέμονο

At last a Greek salad that is more like conventional salads and less like a dip! This is a wonderfully fresh-tasting salad.

serves 4–6

1kg (2¼lb) runner beans
125ml (4fl oz) extra virgin olive oil
2 tbsp lemon juice
1 garlic clove, very finely chopped
salt and pepper to taste
1 bunch fresh basil, leaves only
1 spring onion, trimmed and finely chopped

1 Trim the two ends of the runner beans and peel the sides. Cut the beans into manageable lengths. If, during the peeling, you feel a noisy resistance from the bean, throw it away as it will be stringy.

2 Blanch the beans in boiling salted water for 15 minutes. Drain and plunge into cold water until cold, then drain and transfer to a salad bowl.

3 Make the dressing by whisking the olive oil with the lemon juice and garlic. When the dressing looks well amalgamated, season and pour it over the runner beans. Add the basil leaves and spring onion, then mix.

pan-fried olives

ελιές τηγανητές

The island of Thassos, which lies among the Aegean islands, produces these olives. They may not look as attractive as others, but they have a unique intensity of flavour. If you're lucky enough to be able to take the ferry crossing from Kavala to Thassos in the winter, you will be greeted on arrival by street vendors selling fresh pan-fried local olives. Ouzo would be the only drink to accompany them.

serves 4

150ml (5fl oz) olive oil

1 bunch spring onions, finely chopped

2 whole garlic cloves

400g (14oz) tomato *perasti* (the Greek equivalent of tomato passata)

½ bunch rosemary

finely grated zest of 1 lemon

200g (7oz) stoned Throumbes olives (shrivelled olives)

salt and pepper to taste

1 In a deep frying pan, heat half the olive oil and sauté the spring onions and garlic for 5 minutes. Add the tomato *perasti*, rosemary, and lemon zest, and cook over a low heat for 20–25 minutes. The sauce should be full-bodied by this time and should not look watery.

2 Add the olives and leave the pan over a low heat for another 6–7 minutes. Remove the pan from the heat and let the sauce cool.

3 Stir in the remaining olive oil. Add some freshly ground black pepper and check for salt. If you are not in a hurry, allow the flavours to blend together for a day. Let the dish come to room temperature before serving.

peas and mint

αρακάς Ανωγείων

Fresh peas have the taste of early summer – simple and sweet. It's never quite the same when you tear open a pack of frozen petits pois in the winter! This dish of peas lives on in my imagination as the essence of summer.

serves 6–8

1 bunch fresh mint

2kg (4½lb) fresh peas (after podding there will be 1kg/2¼lb)

250g (9oz) leeks (trimmed weight), finely chopped

1 bunch (about 90g/3¼oz) spring onions, finely chopped

200ml (7fl oz) olive oil

salt and pepper to taste

1 Bind the mint well with butcher's string – you want the flavour, but do not want to pick out the leaves. Put everything into a heavy pot with 1 litre (1¼ pints) of water, cover, and simmer for 1½ hours. The dish is ready when the liquid has nearly gone and there is a pale green, oily sauce.

2 Let the mixture cool well. The flavours will be more appreciated when the dish is eaten at room temperature, or not more than 50°C/122°F. At home we normally eat this with pan-fried calf's liver and plenty of feta cheese.

"An island is a great place to develop a cuisine. Cooks are invariably forced to work with what to the mainlander might seem like a restricted palette, and island cuisine is bound to be seasonal. Great ingenuity is needed to rework the same ingredients and themes time and time again while keeping them fresh."

hilopites with saffron

χυλοπίτες Αστυπάλαιας με ζαφορά

They produce fine saffron on the island of Astypalea, which lies to the south-east of the Cyclades. The locals say that "Saffron grows in gentle valleys, as does life after death".

serves 6

100ml (3½fl oz) olive oil
500g (18oz) shallots
5 garlic cloves
1 x 300g jar tomato *perasti* (the
   Greek equivalent of tomato
   passata)
2 tsp sweet paprika
2 litres (3½ pints) chicken stock,
   plus 1 litre (1¾ pints) water
2 pinches saffron strands
500g (18oz) *hilopites* (or dried
   egg tagliatelle)
100g (3½oz) butter
salt and pepper to taste
1 bunch chives, finely chopped
lots of grated St Michael cheese
   (a very hard cow's milk cheese
   from the island of Syros), or
   Parmesan

1   Preheat the oven to 200°C/400°F/gas mark 6.

2   Put the olive oil, whole shallots, and garlic in a heavy-bottomed non-stick oven dish and place in the oven.

3   After 5–10 minutes, when the garlic and the shallots begin to brown a little, add the tomato *perasti* and sweet paprika. Stir well and return to the oven for 10 minutes.

4   Meanwhile, heat up the chicken stock and water. When hot, add the saffron.

5   Add the *hilopites*, butter, tomato and onion mixture and seasonings to the oven dish, then pour the stock over and return to the oven for 15–20 minutes.

6   Serve the *hilopites* with the chives and plenty of grated St Michael cheese. The dish should have a sloppy, soupy texture.

food from the big city

Life is different in the big city, and so is the food. In metropolitan Athens, where I grew up, our kitchen was home to a host of influences. Dishes may be simple, for instance an artichoke and broad bean salad or the very more-ish cheese triangles, or more ambitious, for instance kid wrapped in vine leaves. Also in this chapter are recipes for *strapatsada* (a kind of superior omelette), chicken cooked with young courgettes, and that classic among classics, a definitive moussaka.

artichoke and broad bean casserole

καλοκαιρινή σαλάτα με αγκινάρες και κουκιά

This dish can serve either as a side dish or, with plenty of crusty bread, as a supper dish. In Greece artichokes are considered to be one of life's little luxuries, as in the proverb "We do not have bread and we want artichokes!".

serves 4

6 large globe artichokes

3 lemons

500ml (18fl oz) dry white wine

150ml (5fl oz) extra virgin olive oil

500g (18oz) firm ripe tomatoes, skinned, seeded, and chopped

3 bunches spring onions, trimmed and finely chopped

1kg (2¼lb) young broad beans, podded

1 bunch dill, finely chopped

1 bunch flat-leaf parsley, destemmed and finely chopped

salt and pepper to taste

1   To prepare the artichokes, cut off the stem to leave about 3cm (1¼in), then peel the stem. Take off the outer two rings of leaves and slice the artichokes across to separate the base from the leaves. Trim it back to reveal the hairy "choke" in the centre of the bud. Remove this carefully with a teaspoon. Each artichoke must be rubbed over with half a lemon, then kept in water that has had lemon juice added to it. The acidulated water stops them oxidizing and going brown.

2   Put the wine in a pan and boil vigorously to drive off the alcohol – this should take 5–7 minutes.

3   Heat the oil in a heavy-bottomed pan, then add the tomatoes, spring onions and reduced wine. Add the artichokes and broad beans and simmer, with the lid on, over a low heat. The artichokes are ready when they're soft to the point of a small knife – this should take 35–45 minutes.

4   Stir in the herbs and adjust the seasoning. Serve lukewarm.

cheese triangles

τυροπιτάκια

To make the filling for these pastries, you can omit the eggs and substitute a half quantity of béchamel sauce. Remember to allow them to cool a little before tucking in, as the cheese inside can burn the mouth even when the outside has cooled to the touch.

serves 8 as mezedes

100g (3½oz) Greek feta cheese

100g (3½oz) Kaseri cheese (a hard cow's milk cheese) or very mature Cheddar

4 medium eggs, or 2 eggs plus ½ recipe quantity béchamel sauce (see page 141, but omit the cheese)

3 heaped tbsp finely chopped mint leaves

½ nutmeg, freshly grated

freshly ground black pepper

500g (18oz) filo pastry

100g (3½oz) butter, melted

250ml (18fl oz) whole milk

100g (3½oz) cold butter

1 Preheat the oven to 180°C/350°F/gas mark 4.

2 Grate the cheeses into a mixing bowl, add two of the eggs and, with a hand blender, turn the mixture into a purée. (Alternatively add the béchamel instead of the eggs to the cheeses and mix thoroughly.) Add the mint, nutmeg, and black pepper, and mix well. The mixture should not need salt as the cheeses are salty enough.

3 Take two sheets of filo, brush one generously with melted butter and lay the other squarely on top. Cut this "sandwich" into strips of approximately 5 x 20cm (2 x 8in). Put 1 tbsp of the cheese filling in the centre of the strip about 2cm (¾in) from the end. Fold one corner over in a triangle. Fold in the edges about 5mm (¼in), then continue turning over the triangle until you reach the end of the filo strip, buttering it well with each turn.

4 Continue making pastries until you have used up all the cheese mixture and arrange them on a baking tray with a rim.

5 Beat the milk with the remaining eggs and pour this liquid over the triangles. Let the tray stand uncovered at room temperature until all the liquid is absorbed.

6 Place a small knob of cold butter on each triangle and bake until they are golden – about 35–40 minutes.

chicken with young courgettes

κοτόπουλο με κολοκυθάκια στην κατσαρόλα

There are times when the conversation at the dinner table falls silent and the only noise is of greedy diners smacking their lips and the occasional contented sigh – then you know the diners may well be eating this dish.

serves 8

2 large chickens (ask your butcher
   to cut them in half and bone
   them out)

juice of 2 lemons

4 garlic cloves, finely chopped

½ bunch mint, finely chopped

salt and pepper to taste

125ml (4fl oz) olive oil

200ml (7fl oz) chicken stock (or
   water)

2 cinnamon sticks

500g (18oz) tomatoes, skinned,
   seeded, and finely chopped

1kg (2¼lb) small courgettes

75ml (2½fl oz) extra virgin olive oil

1   Wash the chickens with lemon juice. Spread the halves on a chopping board, skin side down. Spread the inside evenly with the garlic and mint, and season well. Roll each chicken breast into the thigh – this is important as the breast will cook faster and you need to protect it with the leg meat. Use butcher's string to tie it up in a roll. If this sounds daunting, get your butcher to roll the meat and then apply the flavourings to the outside.

2   Heat 50ml (2fl oz) of the olive oil in a heavy-bottomed pot over a low heat and brown the chicken pieces slowly. It will take about 12 minutes.

3   Add the stock and cinnamon sticks, then simmer for 45 minutes with the lid on. Turn the pieces a couple of times. Top up the stock if it starts to boil dry. When the chicken is cooked through, remove it from the casserole and keep it warm. Discard the cinnamon sticks.

4   Add the tomatoes to the juices in the pan and let them come to the boil. Season, then cook for 10 minutes. Make an incision on both sides of the courgettes. Add them to the pot with the remainder of the olive oil, and cook slowly for 30 minutes. Shake the pot couple of times, as the courgettes can catch. By now the sauce should look quite thick and the courgettes will be very soft. Put the chicken back in the pot and allow everything to cool down.

5   Dress with the extra virgin olive oil before serving at room temperature.

kid wrapped in vine leaves

κατσικάκι με αμπελόφυλλα

This is a spring dish because that is when both vine leaves and young kids are at their most tender. It brings back memories of the etched, brown mountain hills of the island of Astypalea – of standing outside in the morning light as the kids evaded the men trying to catch them, men who seemed to turn darker as the light got stronger.

serves 6

2 kid shoulders, boned (or spring lamb)

juice of 1 lemon

salt and pepper to taste

250g (9oz) potatoes, diced

1 bunch spring onions, trimmed and finely chopped

2 long thin green peppers, seeded and finely diced

250g (9oz) tomatoes, skinned, seeded, and finely chopped

60g (2¼oz) pine nuts

1 bunch dill, finely chopped

150g (5½oz) St Michael cheese (a very hard cow's milk cheese from the island of Syros), or Parmesan, diced

40 tender vine leaves

1   Preheat the oven to 180°C/350°F/gas mark 4.

2   Lay out the two boned shoulders on a chopping board. Rub them with the lemon juice and season well. Set to one side, covered with a damp cloth.

3   Blanch the potatoes in boiling salted water. When they are par-boiled, remove them from the pot and drain.

4   In a large bowl, mix the potatoes with the spring onions, peppers, tomatoes, pine nuts, dill, and cheese. Season.

5   Lay the kid shoulders on the board skin-side-down and spread the potato mixture evenly over the meat. Roll the shoulders up and try to keep all the ingredients inside. Wrap the rolled shoulders with the vine leaves, then wrap again with a few layers of parchment paper. The two individual packets should be tidily wrapped. Finally wrap the parcels in kitchen foil. The better you wrap them, the more moist the kid will be.

6   Roast for 2–3 hours, until the meat is cooked through.

7   Remove from the oven and let the meat cool for about 30 minutes before unwrapping the parcels.

8   Slice the meat, dress it with the cooking juices and eat with a salad of runner beans (see page 125).

rocket, leek and caper pie

πίτα με ρόκα, πράσο και κάπαρη

In our household, we always had this pie on a Tuesday, as that was the day when the street market was held and we could get fresh rocket leaves. The pie should be crisp outside and rich within.

serves 6–8

400g (14oz) rocket, finely chopped

300g (10½oz) leeks, trimmed, washed well, and finely chopped

2 bunches spring onions, finely chopped

1 bunch chervil, finely chopped

1 bunch flat-leaf parsley, finely chopped

400g (14oz) feta cheese

40g (1½oz) Santorinian capers

coarsely ground black pepper

3 eggs, beaten

150g (5½oz) butter, melted, plus extra for greasing

1 x 250g (9oz) pack of filo pastry (or see page 188)

150ml (5fl oz) milk

to serve

strained Greek yoghurt

1   Mix all the greens in a large bowl.

2   Line a large container with a dry kitchen cloth and spread a third of the mixed greens out in it. Arrange further kitchen cloths in further containers and do the same until you have used all the greens. Leave them somewhere cool for an hour: the idea is to get rid of as much water as possible.

3   Preheat the oven to 180°C/350°F/gas mark 4.

4   Break the feta into crumbs, then mix it with the capers and some coarsely ground pepper. Add the greens, then fold in the eggs.

5   Butter the bottom of a spring-release cake tin (23cm/9in in diameter, 7cm/2¾in deep) and line with a generous half of the filo, brushing each sheet heavily with melted butter. Substantial corners of the filo sheets should hang over the tin's edge, as you will need to fold them over to make a top to the pie.

6   Spread in half the greens mixture and top with another two intermediate layers of buttered filo. Spread in the remaining greens mix. Fold the overlapping filo over the surface of the filling, then top with the remaining pastry, buttering each sheet well. You can arrange it decoratively – crumpled, say – on the top. Butter the folded filo and spatter the remaining butter and the milk over the surface. Doing this will make the filo rise in bubbles while the pie is cooking.

7   Bake the pie for 45–60 minutes. Let it rest for 30 minutes before you cut it. Eat with plenty of strained yoghurt.

metropolitan manners

"Athens is like a sluggish horse, and I am the gadfly
trying to sting it into life" (Socrates)

My parents' house in Athens is within sight of the Olympic stadium and, as with so many older Athenian houses, it has a magnificent fig tree in the garden. Figs are bound up with our history and culture, and since ancient times the figs of Attica have been considered the finest in Greece. At one time Athenian figs were so highly prized that they were reserved for Athenians, and export was banned. This led to people smuggling figs out in order to win favours and, as the Greek for fig is "*syco*", anyone accused of this crime became known as a "sycophant".

As well as providing ripe and luscious fruit, the fig tree in our garden was the backdrop to some memorable meals. Several times a year our family would hold big parties, and the garden was the perfect venue. A lot of love and sacrifice goes into my mother's cooking.

At these large affairs, all our friends and neighbours would queue to choose from several dishes. The best party of the year was the one held during the fig season, when my mother made an astonishing pie with mild mountain greens, feta, and a serious quantity of butter (see page 136). This dish is still one of her favourites, as she is always keen to point out that Greek food does not need meat to be savoury. Another classic option would be a moussaka (see page 141) or a roasting tray of lamb with potatoes (see page 100).

However many guests there were, they always ended up seated at a single table. Even if that meant that we, the children, had to be squeezed alongside people we really didn't want to share a seat with. My mother believes that intimacy makes for great conversation and affords a good chance to meet the people across the table.

Slowly the meal would wind its way towards Herculean quantities of dessert: a monster baklava (see page 42) plus plenty of fresh hot *loukoumades* (deep-fried yeast dough dipped in a syrup of honey and spices). Both were served with dollops of thick, strained Greek yoghurt.

My mother doesn't own any cookbooks, but she has an inexhaustible store of traditional recipes, each painstakingly honed over the years, and her knowledge comes with priceless mental "footnotes" dealing with all aspects of choosing, buying, preparing, and serving food. I only have to ask. When I recall some of the dinners she prepared, I think back to my favourite cookbook: the *Deipnosophistai*, *"The Learned Banquet"*, a treatise on food and food preparation written in the second century BC by Athenaeus, a Greek Athenian gourmet. The treatise is presented in the form of a dialogue between two men at a banquet who talk for days and relate recipes for dishes such as stuffed vine leaves and several varieties of cheesecake.

Athens has always been a sophisticated and metropolitan place, but one of the crucial influences upon the city was the integration of the Greeks of Smyrna, nearly all of whom arrived in Athens as refugees during September 1922, when the Turks took over their home town. Before 1922 Smyrna, Marseilles, and Livorno were the three most important cultural ports of the Mediterranean. The immigrants from Smyrna brought with them a strong gastronomic, cultural, artistic, and intellectual awareness.

Athens was a natural choice for their new home, as there was a lot of luxury present in the form of festivals. But this luxury was a function of the city, not individuals, and this is an important distinction. In Athens these festivals and rituals all had their proper place in life and did not overlap with the ordinary events of everyday life. There was a vast difference between life in the privileged Greek communities such as Smyrna and Constantinople, or metropolitan Athens, and life on the islands, where nearly everybody lived in poverty, and sometimes even in destitution.

In addition, when the Athenians started settling down with the new exotic flavours and smells, a new kind of music arrived at our homes. "*Rebetika*", the music of the Greek communities of Asia Minor, is the "soul music" of the refugees. It can be gloomy stuff, as many of the songs deal with death, exile, drug addiction, and love gone wrong. *Rebetika* influenced popular Greek music in much the same way as the American blues influenced rock and roll. Although my father was not fond of this music, my brother and I still have at home a collection full of raw emotion and scratchy 1920s recording quality – a music almost as evocative as my mother's cooking!

moussaka

μουσακάς

During the summer, I only have to catch sight of the moussaka tray and my stomach starts rumbling. And when nothing remains on your plate but the memory of a slice of moussaka, you are left glowing with a great happiness.

serves 8

250ml (9fl oz) vegetable oil

1kg (2¼lb) aubergines, sliced
  lengthways, 1cm thick

500g (18oz) courgettes, sliced
  lengthways, 1cm thick

100ml (3½fl oz) olive oil

250g (9oz) Spanish onions, finely
  chopped

1kg (2¼lb) lamb shoulder, minced

1 tbsp ground cinnamon

salt and pepper to taste

400g (14oz) tomato *perasti* (the
  Greek equivalent of tomato
  passata)

100ml (3½fl oz) red wine, if needed

1 bunch flat-leaf parsley, chopped

béchamel cheese sauce

500–600ml (18–20fl oz) milk

115g (4oz) butter

115g (4oz) plain flour

1 nutmeg, freshly grated

100g (3½oz) Kefalotiri cheese (a
  hard sheep's milk cheese), or
  aged pecorino, grated

2 eggs

1   Heat the vegetable oil in a pan, then fry the vegetables – aubergines first, then the courgettes – turning the slices once. Remove and drain on absorbent kitchen paper.

2   Preheat the oven to 180°C/350°F/gas mark 4.

3   In a heavy-bottomed frying pan, heat the olive oil. Sauté the onions until soft. Add the minced meat and cook until well browned, keeping the heat low. Add the ground cinnamon, some salt and pepper, and the tomato *perasti*. Stir well and, if the mixture looks slightly dry, add red wine. Simmer with the lid on for 20–30 minutes, or until the meat sauce is well cooked and the liquid has been absorbed. It is important to keep stirring, as you do not want to end up with a lumpy sauce.

4   In a roasting tray, make alternate layers of aubergine and courgette slices, meat sauce, and parsley. Start and finish with aubergine slices.

5   To make the béchamel sauce, heat the milk to just below boiling point. In another pan, melt the butter, add the flour, and stir over a low heat until well blended and slightly coloured. This will take almost 5 minutes. Then add the hot milk a little at a time, stirring continually to ensure lumps do not form. Season well and add the nutmeg. Simmer until the sauce thickens. To make the béchamel sauce a cheese sauce, add the grated cheese, stir well, and remove the pan from the heat. After 20 minutes, beat the eggs thoroughly and stir them into the sauce.

6   Pour the sauce over the minced meat and aubergines, and bake for about 1 hour. It is ready when the top of the sauce is brown and has a crust. Let it rest for 1 hour, then serve with a tomato salad.

strapatsada

στραπατσάδα

This is a seriously good egg dish that most closely resembles a Spanish omelette. Wholesome and hearty.

serves 4

1kg (2¼lb) ripe tomatoes

2 green peppers, seeded and finely chopped

½ bunch oregano, finely chopped

salt and pepper to taste

8 eggs

500g (18oz) good feta cheese

100ml (3½fl oz) olive oil

1 bunch basil, torn up

1 Skin the tomatoes by dropping them into boiling water for a few seconds, then skinning them, and chop finely. Place in a deep frying pan with the peppers, the oregano, plenty of coarsely ground black pepper, and some salt (not too much if the feta you are using is salty). Cook gently until the liquid from the tomatoes is reduced and no longer looks watery.

2 Beat the eggs together in a bowl. Crumble the feta into small lumps. Add the oil, cheese, eggs, and basil to the tomato mixture. Cook gently, stirring continuously with a wooden spoon, until the eggs are done.

feta and roast garlic turnovers

ηπειρώτικα πιτάκια τηγανητά

The end of September was highlighted in red on my dad's calendar. After checking his cholesterol level he would be off to Metsovo on a week-long trip to arrange the next year's feta supplies for his delicatessen. His order could be as many as 2,000 beechwood barrels, each containing 50kg (112lb) of cheese! On his return my mother would make these little pies.

makes about 48 turnovers

100ml (3½fl oz) olive oil
6 garlic cloves
½ bunch rosemary
500g (18oz) feta cheese, crumbled
black pepper
900g (2lb) shortcrust pastry
2 eggs beaten with 1 tbsp milk, for egg wash
100g (3½oz) fine semolina
groundnut oil for frying

1 Put the olive oil, garlic, and rosemary in a small saucepan and infuse over low heat until the garlic is soft – about 20 minutes. Strain the oil and let it cool down, saving the cooked garlic.

2 Mash the feta and garlic together and moisten with 1 tbsp of the infused oil. Add some black pepper.

3 Roll out the pastry thinly into pieces about 5cm (2in) wide and 10cm (4in) long. Brush each strip with the infused olive oil and arrange 2 tsp cheese mixture to one side of the centre line. Wet the edge with a little water, fold over, and crimp the edges of the pastry as if you were making a small pasty. When all the little pies are done, brush them with the egg wash and sprinkle with semolina.

4 Heat the groundnut oil in a shallow frying pan, but don't let it reach smoking point. Shallow-fry the little pies, turning them over continually so that the semolina doesn't burn. It is very important to avoid getting the oil too hot. If you notice the oil is getting dirty, discard it and use fresh.

5 Serve with *taratori* (see page 174).

yiouverlakia soup

γιουβαρλάκια

If you don't want to make the avgolemono*, you can simply eat this soup with its meatballs. Just add a few drops of lemon juice.*

serves 6 (makes about 30 meatballs)

250g (9oz) lean pork mince
½ white onion, finely diced
½ bunch spring onions, finely diced
55g (2oz) short-grain rice
½ bunch flat-leaf parsley, very finely chopped
½ bunch mint, very finely chopped
salt and pepper to taste
3 eggs
1 litre (1¾ pints) chicken stock
juice of 2 lemons
1 bunch dill, finely chopped

1   In a large bowl, combine the meat, onion, spring onion, rice, parsley, mint, salt and pepper, and one of the eggs. Knead for a few minutes, then shape into walnut-sized meatballs and set aside.

2   In a large soup pot, bring the stock to the boil. Lower the heat and add the meatballs. Simmer, covered, for 30–40 minutes, then remove the pot from the heat.

3   For the *avgolemono*, beat the remaining egg whites in a bowl for 2 minutes. Continue to beat as you add 250ml (9fl oz) of the stock from the main pot a little at a time, then beat in the lemon juice. Add the egg yolks and continue whisking for a couple more minutes.

4   Return the mixture to the soup and heat very gently. Serve hot, garnished with the dill.

lemon and dill bread

αθηναϊκό ψωμί με ξύσμα λεμονιού και άνηθο

This is not a commonplace bread. The baker that our family uses in Athens tends to make these more exotic loaves when she has a glut of dill in her garden.

makes 3 loaves

300g (10½oz) strong white flour

100g (3½oz) rye flour

100g (3½oz) fine semolina

2 tsp salt

2 tsp caster sugar

25g (1oz) fresh yeast

25g (1oz) cold butter, finely diced

1 bunch dill, finely chopped

finely grated zest of 1½ lemons

olive oil for greasing

1 egg mixed with 2 tbsp milk for
    egg wash

3 tbsp sesame seeds

1   Put the flours, semolina, salt, sugar, yeast, butter, and 300ml (10fl oz) of water at 28–30°C/82–86°F into the bowl of your food mixer.

2   Using the dough hook, or kneading attachment, let the motor run on a low speed for 6 minutes, then increase the speed. Knead for 10 minutes. Add the dill and lemon zest, and leave the motor running for 5 more minutes.

3   Remove the bowl from the mixer, cover the dough with a damp cloth and let it prove in a warm place for 1½ hours.

4   Preheat the oven to 220°C/425°F/gas mark 7.

5   Knock back the raised dough by hand, divide into three equal pieces of approximately 275g (9½oz), and shape them into oval loaves. Place on an oiled baking sheet and allow to prove for 30 minutes.

6   Brush the tops with the egg wash, sprinkle with the sesame seeds and place in the oven. Spray the top of the loaves and the oven with water. After 10 minutes, turn the oven down to 200°C/400°F/gas mark 6. Bake for 20 minutes more.

7   Remove the loaves from the oven and cool on a rack.

food for fishermen

Greeks love the sea, and I pine for it if I'm trapped inland. With all fish cookery "simple is good", and fresh ingredients should be allowed to speak for themselves. Fishermen turn to honest dishes such as baked fish with fennel and leeks, marinated fresh anchovies, octopus with button onions and, for more extravagant occasions, barbecued lobster with parsley spread. Then, for times when the winter storms rage, there are preserved fish dishes such as salt cod with shallots.

stewed squid with horta

καλαμάρια κατσαρόλας με χόρτα του βουνού

Every year, on the first weekend after our National Day – 28th October – my mother would put us to work cleaning the barbecue and storing it away in the shed. For us our National Day signalled the end of grilled food for the year. When we had put the barbecue away, we had to unpack all the casseroles for winter and check which ones needed re-coppering.

serves 4

1kg (2¼lb) cleaned squid (about 2kg/4½lb unprepared; ask your fishmonger to help)
200ml (7fl oz) olive oil
1kg (2¼lb) shallots, peeled
20g (¾oz) garlic cloves, peeled
1.5kg (3lb 5oz) *horta* (fresh greens like spinach)
salt and pepper to taste
300g (10½oz) tomato *perasti* (the Greek equivalent of tomato passata)

1 Cut the squid into manageable chunks – about 4cm (1¹/2in) square – then crisscross score one side.

2 Put the olive oil, shallots, and garlic in a large saucepan over a very low heat and braise with the lid on. In about 30 minutes the shallots and garlic will be melting, but not coloured.

3 Add the *horta*, stir well, and leave to cook with the lid on for another 30 minutes. Season and add the tomato *perasti*. By this time, there should be some liquid in the pan. If your pan looks dry, you have been using too strong a heat.

4 Add the squid, stir well, replace the lid, and cook for 20–30 minutes, until the squid is tender. Adjust the seasoning. The dish is ready when the juices taste strongly of squid. Do not plate straight away, but allow it to rest for 10–15 minutes.

5 Lovers of extra virgin olive oil will drizzle a couple of tbsp over their meal. Warm bread is an essential accompaniment.

barbecued lobster with parsley spread

αστακός στα κάρβουνα με σάλτσα μαϊντανού

This is one of the dishes that I cooked while on a magnificent sailing yacht called Larne. We spent a magical night anchored in Scandia bay on the island of Kythera. After we finished the lobsters we sat in the inky night under the stars.

serves 4

4 live lobsters, approx. 500g
   (18oz) each
1 green pepper, seeded and
   finely chopped
1 bunch chives, finely chopped
50ml (2fl oz) olive oil
2 tbsp runny honey
juice and finely grated zest of
   1 lemon

parsley spread

125g (4½oz) stale bread
1 generous bunch flat-leaf parsley,
   including stalks, finely chopped
½ bunch spring onions, chopped
1 egg yolk
150ml (5fl oz) extra virgin olive oil
juice of 1 lemon
salt and pepper to taste

1   First make the parsley spread. Rinse the bread under a tap until soggy, then squeeze out the excess water. Pulse the parsley and spring onions in the food processor. Crumble the bread and add it to the food processor bowl, pulsing on and off as it combines. The locals would add a couple of preserved anchovies while the processor is running.

2   Add the egg yolk and pulse on and off a few times. Slowly drizzle in the olive oil and lemon juice, pulsing until the mixture is smooth and creamy. Season to taste with salt and pepper.

3   When you buy your lobsters, make sure that they have all their legs and claws, and are lively. To kill the lobsters mercifully, stab them through the cross in the centre of their head. Then cut each in half lengthways. Remove the digestive tract and the grey sac you will find in the head. Crack the claws with the back of a knife.

4   Mix all the remaining ingredients together for a marinade in a large bowl. Place the lobsters in a suitable container and pour the marinade over them. Cover and place them in the refrigerator for 30–60 minutes before cooking.

5   Preheat the barbecue or domestic grill.

6   Place the lobsters (and their claws) flesh side down on a barbecue. Cook the lobsters for 5–8 minutes on each side. Alternatively, cook under a hot grill. The lobsters are ready when the shells turn red. The flesh should be pink and white.

7   As the lobsters come off the barbecue, spread each generously with the parsley mixture and eat while they are still warm.

salt cod with shallots

νησιώτικος μπακαλιάρος

When you tie up your sailing boat in a deserted bay at Mani, it feels as if every olive tree has been there for hundreds of years. While everything else is subject to change, this landscape is permanent. After a day in the heat, it is the ideal setting for a cool glass of retsina and this dish, which originates in the fishing port of Kalamata.

serves 6

1kg (2¼lb) salt cod fillets
200ml (7fl oz) olive oil
500g (18oz) whole shallots
2 bay leaves
500g (18oz) ripe tomatoes,
  skinned, seeded and coarsely
  chopped
plain flour for dipping
salt and pepper to taste

1 Soak the salt cod overnight in enough water to cover the fillets. Change the water a couple of times before you go to bed and you will get a better result. The next day, remove the cod from the water, skin and remove any pin bones, then rinse and dry it.

2 Gently heat half the olive oil in a shallow casserole. Add the shallots and bay leaves, cover with the lid, and braise over a low heat for 15 minutes.

3 Add the tomatoes to the shallots. Continue to cook over a low heat for 40 minutes.

4 Add the remaining olive oil to the pot. Dip the salt cod fillets in flour, then add them as well. Cover the pot and cook until the liquid is absorbed and only the oil remains – about 20 minutes. Add black pepper and check for salt. Be careful, as the dish will taste saltier later, when the sauce absorbs some salt from the cod.

5 Remove from the heat and allow the cod to cool down in the casserole. Serve at room temperature.

baked fish with fennel and leeks

ψάρι στον φούρνο με μάραθο και πράσα

This dish is a family favourite. It is not fancy or difficult, but it touches a chord. For my mother, flavours such as these have served to bind our family together even though we are dispersed.

serves 6

250ml (9fl oz) olive oil
500g (18oz) fennel bulb, with any
   feathery leaves, finely chopped
700g (1lb 9oz) leeks, trimmed
   and finely chopped
1 bunch spring onions, trimmed
   and finely chopped
500g (18oz) tomatoes, skinned,
   seeded, and finely chopped
salt and pepper to taste
1kg (2¼lb) fish fillets (any fresh,
   firm, white-fleshed fish), pin boned

1 Preheat the oven to 200°C/400°F/gas mark 6.

2 Heat 100ml (3½fl oz) of the olive oil in a deep saucepan, then add the fennel, leeks, and spring onions, and sauté. After a few minutes they will take on some colour. Add the tomatoes and season well. Keep simmering until everything has thickened.

3 Spread the mixture onto a roasting tray. Arrange the fish fillets on top in a single layer, season well, and sprinkle with another 100ml (3½fl oz) of the olive oil. Bake for 15 minutes, until the fish is cooked through.

4 Remove from the oven and let the fish cool down for 10 minutes. Dress with the remaining olive oil if you like the raw flavour of olive oil on cooked fish.

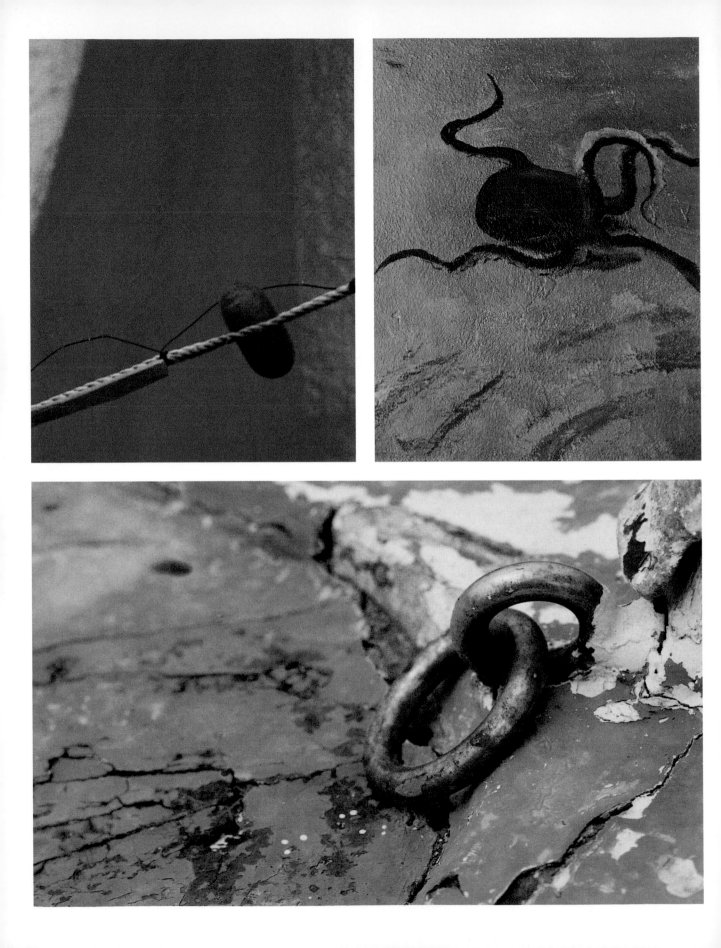

cuttlefish and potatoes

σουπιές με πατάτες

Cuttlefish are similar creatures to squid, but they are thicker and more meaty. A large cuttlefish – which you get in the spring – has a texture that is almost like beef steak.

serves 4

1kg (2¼lb) cuttlefish (or squid),
   cleaned and prepared well
50ml (2fl oz) olive oil
salt and pepper to taste
100ml (3½fl oz) white wine
200g (7oz) *akrokolion* (a
   wonderful Greek dried ham) or
   prosciutto, finely sliced

potatoes

100ml (3½fl oz) olive oil
500g (18oz) whole button onions
500g (18oz) ripe tomatoes, skinned,
   seeded, and coarsely chopped
1kg (2¼lb) potatoes, cut into
   large pieces
finely grated zest of 1 lemon

dressing

100ml (3½fl oz) extra virgin olive oil
25g (1oz) Corinthian sultanas,
   soaked in 50ml (2fl oz) red
   wine vinegar until plump
1 bunch basil, shredded

1 To prepare the potatoes, heat the olive oil in a saucepan, then sauté the button onions for 10 minutes with the lid on and over a low heat. Add the tomatoes and cook for 5 minutes more before adding the potatoes. Simmer until the potatoes are soft and the sauce has reduced and thickened – about 20 minutes. Use the lowest heat you can. When the potatoes are just ready, remove the pot from the heat, add the lemon zest, and adjust the seasoning. Set the pot aside to rest with the lid on.

2 Take your cuttlefish and separate the tentacles before cutting the body into large strips. Sauté in the olive oil, adding salt and pepper to taste. Pour in the wine and simmer with the lid on until soft – about 20 minutes if you are using cuttlefish or 10 minutes for squid.

3 For the dressing, pour the extra virgin olive oil, sultanas and red wine vinegar into a jar, put the lid on, and shake well. Mix in the basil and and adjust the seasoning.

4 To assemble the dish, first arrange the potatoes on a platter, then the cuttlefish, then the *akrokolion* on top. Finally pour the dressing over everything.

octopus with button onions

χταπόδι στιφάδο

The best place to catch octopuses is in an area of sea where there are plenty of rocks: every crevice may hold an octopus. On a sandy bottom, the magnificent camouflage of the octopus makes it hard to spot. When you catch your octopus, you must kill it immediately or else it will start to bite off its own tentacles in order to escape. Traditionally fishermen kill an octopus by biting it between the eyes!

serves 4

4 tsp olive oil

2kg (4½lb) octopus, legs
  separated from the head

500g (18oz) button onions

200g (7oz) Greek tomato *perasti*
  (the Greek equivalent of
  tomato passata)

50ml (2fl oz) extra virgin olive oil

1   Place a large, empty, heavy-bottomed casserole on the stove for 5 minutes to get hot. Add the olive oil and throw the octopus into the pot. Cover and turn the heat down as low as possible. When the octopus is tender, (about 1½ hours later), remove it from the pot and cut into chunks. Place it in a bowl and keep warm.

2   Add the button onions to the octopus juices and cook until they are done, but still have some bite – about 40 minutes. Add the tomato *perasti* and heat gently for a few minutes. Pour the sauce over the octopus, add the extra virgin olive oil, and let everything cool down together so the flavours mingle. This dish should be served at room temperature.

the velvet night

All the bougainvillea flowers point towards silence,
All the eyes towards the August full moon,
And so the confidences unwind,
Drifting up towards the star of Aphrodite.

fresh anchovies in a simple marinade

γαύρος μαρινάτος

These little fish taste great and teach us the valuable lesson that the dishes that taste the best are not necessarily those that require the most skills.

serves 4

500g (18oz) fresh anchovies (you could substitute small sardines)

4 garlic cloves, thinly sliced

250ml (9fl oz) aged Corinthian red wine vinegar

2 tbsp sea salt

50ml (2fl oz) extra virgin olive oil

1 bunch flat-leaf parsley, finely chopped

1   Behead all the anchovies. Grasp the top of each backbone, then give it a sharp jerk away from the meat and it will come free, bringing the little bones with it. This should leave two fillets of meat linked at the tail end.

2   Wash the fish and place in a single layer in a shallow dish. Arrange the garlic on top. Add enough vinegar to cover and sprinkle with the sea salt.

3   Marinate for between 6 and 24 hours, or until the fillets have turned white and firmed up – this shows that they have been "cooked" by the vinegar. Personally I don't leave them in the marinade for more than 6 hours, as I like them less vinegary than some.

4   Drain the anchovies, rinse in cold water, and arrange on a serving plate. Dress with the olive oil and parsley.

5   Eat with a courgette salad (see page 169) and numerous Santorinian tomato *keftedes* (see page 66).

seafood saganaki

σαγανάκι του ψαρά

The art of cooking and eating is mysterious, and recipes evolve to suit their surroundings and the cook. This dish works best when you have spanking fresh seafood to make it with, and the sun setting in the sea to look at while you are eating. Be pragmatic and substitute whatever shellfish you can get hold of.

serves 6

100ml (3½fl oz) olive oil

24 button onions

3 plum tomatoes, skinned, seeded, and finely chopped

3 garlic cloves, finely chopped

a few celery leaves

12 live clams (palourdes are best), cleaned and prepared

24 mussels (rope-grown for choice), cleaned and prepared

200g (7oz) feta cheese, cut into large dice

12 raw large uncooked prawns (shells and heads on)

6 large scallops (live and diver caught if possible), shelled, prepared, and cleaned

50ml (2fl oz) ouzo

salt and pepper to taste

1 bunch flat-leaf parsley, finely chopped

50ml (2fl oz) extra virgin olive oil

1   In a large, heavy-bottomed frying pan, heat half the olive oil. Add the button onions, tomatoes, garlic, and celery leaves and simmer for 10 minutes.

2   Add the cleaned and prepared clams and mussels, put the lid on and cook over a low heat for a further 5 minutes, or until the mussels and clams have opened. Discard any that do not open (unless substituting frozen shellfish). Add the feta and remove the pan from the heat.

3   In another frying pan, heat the remaining olive oil and sear the prawns, then the scallops. Flambé the pan with the ouzo and pour everything into the pot containing the mussels and clams.

4   Cook everything together gently for 5 more minutes. Remove from the heat, season, and sprinkle with the parsley and extra virgin olive oil. Sunset or not, eat this dish while it is still hot, with plenty of fresh bread!

essential recipes for greek home cooking

Most Greek meals start slowly with a few *mezedes* and then wind their way happily through numerous courses. Here you'll find the best of the dips, snacks, breads, salads, and other essentials. These include taramosalata, *tzatziki*, courgette salad, pan-fried feta, *imam bayeldi*, plus a basic *avgolemono* sauce, a recipe for making your own filo pastry, and a really yummy chicken soup with lemon and rice.

taramasalata

ταραμοσαλάτα

Once "tarama" was reserved for "clean Monday" and Lent, but now taramasalata has become the archetypal Greek dish. To make a good taramasalata, use the tarama paste that you can get from Greek shops, which guarantees a strong taste. You can use cod's roe, but the tarama paste works better.

serves 12 as mezedes

40g (1½oz) crustless sliced white bread

200g (7oz) *tarama* paste or cod's roe

200ml (7fl oz) olive oil (or half half olive and half vegetable oil)

40ml (1½fl oz) freshly squeezed lemon juice

1   Soak the crustless bread slices briefly in water, then squeeze them until almost dry. Skin the cod's roe if using, and break it up into chunks.

2   Put the bread, *tarama* paste or cod's roe, and oil into a bowl and use a hand-held electric mixer to amalgamate them. Start very slowly, building up speed gradually, adding the lemon juice and 50ml (2fl oz) warm water. Alternatively just work the ingredients together well with a wooden spoon. If the mixture seems too stiff, add a little more warm water.

tzatziki

τζατζίκι

Use thick Greek yoghurt if possible, and remember that tzatziki becomes stronger and more acidic the longer you keep it.

serves 8 as mezedes

1 cucumber
250g (9oz) thick Greek yoghurt
2 tbsp extra virgin olive oil
1 garlic clove, crushed
1 tbsp finely chopped mint
salt and pepper to taste

1 Peel, seed, and finely dice the cucumber. Be careful to get rid of all the seeds, as they will make the finished *tzatziki* watery.

2 Mix the cucumber with the yoghurt, oil, garlic, and mint. Season to taste with salt and pepper. Refrigerate, covered, for at least a day to let the flavours develop.

sweet pepper purée

πάστα με γλυκές πιπεριές

There is no point in trying to make this recipe in the winter. Think of summer, think of a slow and laid-back life, then think of how nice it will be to play back some of those hot summer memories during the cold miserable days of winter.

serves 12 as mezedes

1kg (2¼lb) sweet red peppers, halved and seeded

salt and pepper to taste

500g (18oz) ripe tomatoes

2 garlic cloves, very finely sliced

1 bunch thyme, leaves only

1 long chilli pepper, halved and seeded

100ml (3½fl oz) extra virgin olive oil (if preserving the purée)

1   Preheat the oven to 190°C/375°F/gas mark 5.

2   Place all the peppers flat in a roasting tray, sprinkle them with sea salt, and bake for half an hour. Take them out of the oven, cool a little, and remove the skins while they are still warm.

3   Cut the tomatoes in half and put them on a cooling rack in a roasting tin with the cut flesh looking up at you. Arrange the garlic on each and sprinkle the thyme and sea salt generously over them. Snuggle the chilli peppers in between the tomatoes. Leave them in the warm on the top of the Aga or in a cool oven (60°C/140°F/the lowest gas), overnight.

4   The next day, put all the peppers and tomatoes in a liquidizer and turn them into a thick, runny paste. Refrigerate, covered. This stuff is amazing and can be used as a dip for chips or with cold meats.

5   You can preserve the purée by spreading the paste back onto the roasting tray and putting it back in the oven at the same very low temperature. Leave for 8–12 hours as convenient. Alternatively (weather permitting), cover the roasting tray with cheesecloth and place it out in the blazing sun for a day!

6   Mix the (now dehydrated) purée well and place it in a pickling jar with a lid on. Pour the extra virgin olive oil on top of the purée and keep in the refrigerator.

courgette salad

σαλάτα με κολοκυθάκια

In Greece, the finest courgettes are picked small and are prized as highly as more exalted vegetables such as asparagus. By the time the sun had risen my mother would be coming back with a basket full of these tender little marrows, as she believed they were at their best before dawn.

serves 4

1kg (2¼lb) small courgettes
5 garlic cloves, thinly sliced
salt and pepper to taste
100ml (3½fl oz) extra virgin olive oil
juice of 1 lemon
½ bunch flat-leaf parsley, very
  finely chopped

1   Preheat the oven to 180°C/350°F/gas mark 4.

2   Wash the courgettes. With a paring knife, make a cut along 80 per cent of the length of each courgette, leaving the two ends uncut or they may split open. Slip the garlic into the slits.

3   Arrange the courgettes in a heavy-bottomed casserole, making sure that they do not overlap. Season and add 100ml (3½fl oz) water and half the olive oil. Put the lid on and bake for 30 minutes. Turn them over and put them back in the oven for another 30 minutes.

4   Remove the courgettes from the oven, take the lid off, and let them cool down. When at room temperature, whisk the remaining extra virgin olive oil with the lemon juice and pour it over the courgettes.

5   Add the parsley and eat as an accompaniment or as a dish in its own right.

skordalia with walnuts
σκορδαλιά με καρύδια

The story goes that Kapodistrias, the first leader of independent Greece, met a French girl in Paris who was a chef and who would indulge him with potage parmentier *and* pommes de terre dauphinoise. *When he settled in Nafplio, which was the first capital of Greece, he tried to give away potatoes to the local people, who were somewhat put off by his description: "As a vegetable, the potato is content with its poison until your saliva turns it into fragrance!" That goes for this rich potato dip!*

serves 12 as mezedes

500g (18oz) potatoes, washed
salt and pepper to taste
½ garlic bulb
400ml (14fl oz) olive oil (up to
  500ml/18fl oz)
juice of 1 lemon
2 tsp white wine vinegar
75g (2¾oz) shelled walnuts, finely
  chopped
2 egg yolks

1   Place the potatoes in a pot with plenty of water and some salt, and boil them with their skins still on.

2   Mash the garlic completely (you can use the food processor).

3   When the potatoes are cooked, drain the water and peel them while they are hot. Put the potatoes in a mixer and use the whisk attachment to mash them, one by one, until you have a purée. Add the garlic, then the olive oil, lemon juice, and vinegar by turns, beating constantly. If the sauce is too thick for your taste, add a little hot water. Add the walnuts and egg yolks, and keep mixing. This dip shouldn't be lumpy.

htipiti

ΧΤΥΠΗΤή

Be careful to maintain the rough texture of this Thracian meze, *and to use the best barrel-aged feta cheese if possible.*

serves 8 as mezedes

125g (4½oz) red onions

75ml (2½fl oz) extra virgin olive oil

350g (12oz) red peppers
   (sometimes available ready
   roasted in jars)

300g (10½oz) good feta cheese

2 tbsp white wine vinegar

1 tsp chopped parsley

1 tsp thyme leaves

salt and pepper to taste

1   Preheat the oven to 200°C/400°F/gas mark 6.

2   Peel the onions and put them on a baking tray. Drizzle with 4 tsp of the oil and roast for about 45 minutes, or until soft.

3   If you are preparing your own peppers, wrap each one in foil and roast them for 30 minutes. When cooked, cool a little then rub off the skins while they are still hot.

4   Chop the peppers and onions finely and mash together with the cheese. Mix in the remaining oil, the vinegar, parsley, and thyme. The perfect texture is similar to that of a coarse meat paste. Season to taste.

pan-fried feta

φέτα σαγανάκι

Start by sourcing the best Greek feta cheese that you can find – look for the words "barrel-aged".

serves 4 as mezedes

55g (2oz) unsalted butter

4 tbsp vegetable oil

300g (10½oz) feta cheese, cut
  into narrow fingers

iced water

plain flour, seasoned with salt and
  pepper

1 Heat the butter and oil together in a frying pan.

2 Put the cheese fingers in a bowl of iced water for 30 seconds. This will make the flour stick and help form the crust.

3 Roll the cheese in the seasoned flour and fry until crisp and golden on the outside and melting on the inside. Serve promptly.

taratori

ταρατούρι Ηπείρου

Florina in northern Greece is well known for its amazing red peppers. At the end of the summer, the town smells of wood-burning barbecues, all of which seem to be covered with red peppers. When the peppers are ready, they are pickled in jars with a solution of vinegar and sugar. When I was a child, there was the added thrill of maybe finding a worm in your portion – pickled by now like the pepper in which it had made its home.

serves 12 as mezedes

100g (3½oz) red peppers,
  preserved in a jar (from Florina
  if possible)
sea salt and pepper to taste
1 bunch spring onions, trimmed
  and finely chopped
250g (9oz) strained Greek yoghurt
30g (1¼oz) garlic cloves, finely
  chopped
1 cucumber, peeled, seeded,
  and finely diced
½ bunch dill, finely chopped
½ bunch mint, finely chopped
2 tbsp extra virgin olive oil

1   Drain the peppers, cut in half, seed, and roughly purée with the back of a knife on a board.

2   In a small bowl, add a bit of sea salt to the spring onions, mix well with your fingers, then rinse. This will remove some of the oniony smell and make the flavour less harsh.

3   In a large bowl, combine all the ingredients well. Taste and adjust the seasoning. Keep the mixture refrigerated, covered, until needed.

4   Before serving, stir some ice cubes into the mixture: as they start to melt, the mixture will become authentically runny, the way they eat it in Epirus. You can eat it with a spoon.

cheese and garlic spread

τυροσαλάτα με σκόρδο

This keeps well in the refrigerator and is delicious spread thickly on tomatoes or crusty bread. Do not throw away the thyme-infused oil, as it is great for dipping bread into or for frying eggs.

serves 12 as mezedes

4 garlic cloves

50ml (2fl oz) olive oil

½ bunch thyme

300g (10½oz) Cretan cream
cheese (or a soft and creamy
goat's cheese)

finely grated zest of 1 lemon

2 tbsp extra virgin olive oil

1 Place the garlic, olive oil, and thyme in a small pan and cook gently over a low heat for about 30 minutes with the lid on. Remove the pan from the heat and let it cool down.

2 Place the softened garlic in a mixing bowl with the cheese, lemon zest, and extra virgin olive oil, and mix together well. Alternatively, place all these ingredients in a food processor and blitz on a slow speed until smooth.

cheese spread

τυροσαλάτα

The perfect bread for this spread is rye bread or good sourdough. Cut a thick slice, spread it with butter, and toast it on a griddle pan. While it is still hot, spread generously with the cheese spread and eat it before it has a chance to go cold. You could substitute pecorino or provolone cheeses, but it rather misses the point!

serves 12 as mezedes

100g (3½oz) Manouri cheese (a soft whey cheese made from ewe's milk)

100g (3½oz) Kaseri cheese (a semi-hard ewe's milk cheese)

40g (1½oz) strained Greek yoghurt

1 Grate the cheeses, put them in a liquidizer with the yoghurt, and blitz until you have a fine cheesy paste.

2 This will keep in the refrigerator, covered, for a long time.

first things last

When we were children, if my parents went out and left us alone, I always ended up doing the cooking, but somehow my version of each dish would never quite equal my mother's. "I must show you how to cook, Theodore," she would say upon her return. But she never got around to formal lessons. She did, however, give me the best culinary insight that I have ever received. My mother would peel oranges, roast the fruit in the fireplace, boil the skin with water and sugar, then give me a roasted orange and the strange bittersweet drink. Her intention was to make me more courageous about food and drink. From her standpoint, intensity of flavour (and of every experience) was of paramount importance. Going home to Greece to work on this book was a return to such intensity, and it still had the power to move me. One of my mother's favourite sayings is: "Food and paintings wear away, the familiar smells and colours seep into the eyes of the people enjoying them, until one day they start to fade away. But never let them vanish. For the ones who let them vanish, jail is the only place!"

The memories were particularly strong on the island of Evoia, at the outdoor dining table presided over by Aunty Argini, a woman with a locket at her throat and vivid eyes that nettled all newcomers. Deep within the olive grove at the agricultural cooperative called Rovies, Argini and Koula, two accomplished and instinctive cooks, would prepare an endless parade of seasonal dishes without making any big fuss about it. Koula would continually exhort the diners "Keep awake, keep awake, do not give in to only one dish. You are my hostages and prisoners of my cooking flavours!"

Ouzo is the main drink during the preparation of food. It is the Greek national drink, only made in Greece. Ouzo is made from a combination of pressed grapes, herbs, and berries. Starting as a clear alcohol, when it is mixed with water it turns whitish and opaque. This is because ouzo is made with anise seed, and when anise oil is combined with water it turns into white crystals that are opaque. Aunty Argini would have it that ouzo drinking is an art, and maybe also a way of life. But it's not the ouzo that counts – it's who you drink it with. Ouzo tastes best when it is drunk at home and is a merry catalyst for good times, but the key to drinking ouzo is to eat *mezedes* with it. The *mezedes* that Koula made varied from an artichoke salad with dill, taramasalata, cured fresh anchovies with herbs and garlic, and pickled aubergines with celery leaves, to meatballs, *souvlaki* with all its trimmings, fine cheeses from Crete, and of course mountains of *loukoumades* with thyme honey and strained yoghurt. All had intense flavours to keep the effects of the alcohol from overwhelming us and to enable us to sit and drink slowly for hours in that calm state of mind where all is beautiful and life is fine.

Moreover, even without ouzo, life in Rovies is slow and beautiful, and it is easy to lose all sense of time. An hour seemed like a week, and suddenly a whole week went by as if we had dreamed it. Sitting around the table with Aunty Argini's family and some of the workers from the olive grove was the best way to get to the essence of things. Long after sunset we would sit around the outdoor table once more surrounded by a strange silence filled with stories; silence throbbing with the olive grove's sounds, screeching and murmurs, and the odd fox coming closer to the veranda in case anyone was generous enough to share some of the food with her. Those are the images that I miss when back in London, but thankfully just trying the recipes brings them flooding back.

imam bayeldi

ιμάμ μπαϊλντί

This dish should be sinfully rich, and there is an apocryphal tale that the name derived from the holy man who fainted when he first tasted it. Some say he fainted because the dish was so rich, and some that he fainted at the thought of spending all that money on oil...

serves 6 as mezedes

1kg (2¼lb) large aubergines (at
   least 12cm/4½in long, if
   possible thin rather than fat)
100ml (3½fl oz) olive oil
1kg (2¼lb) Spanish onions, thinly
   sliced
2 tsp caster sugar
200g (7oz) plum tomatoes,
   skinned, seeded, and sliced
3 heaped tbsp finely chopped
   flat-leaf parsley
3 garlic cloves, thinly sliced
salt and pepper to taste

1   Peel half the skin off the aubergines in long strips so that they look stripy. With the tip of a paring knife, make a deep slash lengthways in each aubergine. Sprinkle them with salt and allow them to stand for 30 minutes, then rinse.

2   Preheat the oven to 170–180°C/325–350°F/gas mark 3–4.

3   Gently heat half the olive oil in a frying pan, then add the onions and sugar, and cook very slowly for about an hour until they are completely soft.

4   Spread a third of the fried onions over the base of an oiled casserole dish. Add a layer of tomatoes and put to one side.

5   Add the remaining tomatoes and half the parsley to the fried onions in the frying pan. Mix well and cook for 10 minutes.

6   Add 2 tbsp water to the mixture in the frying pan and stir. Arrange the aubergines on the onion mixture in the bottom of the casserole and, using a spoon, stuff the garlic into the slits in the aubergines. Add the tomato and onion mixture from the frying pan, attempting to work it into the slashes as well. It should overflow!

7   Season well and pour over the remaining oil. Cover the casserole with a sheet of foil and put the lid on. This should ensure a good seal.

8   Bake for 40 minutes, or until the aubergines are soft. If you like a thick sauce, remove the lid for the last 10 minutes to allow it to dry off a little.

9   Allow to cool to lukewarm, then sprinkle with the remaining parsley and serve.

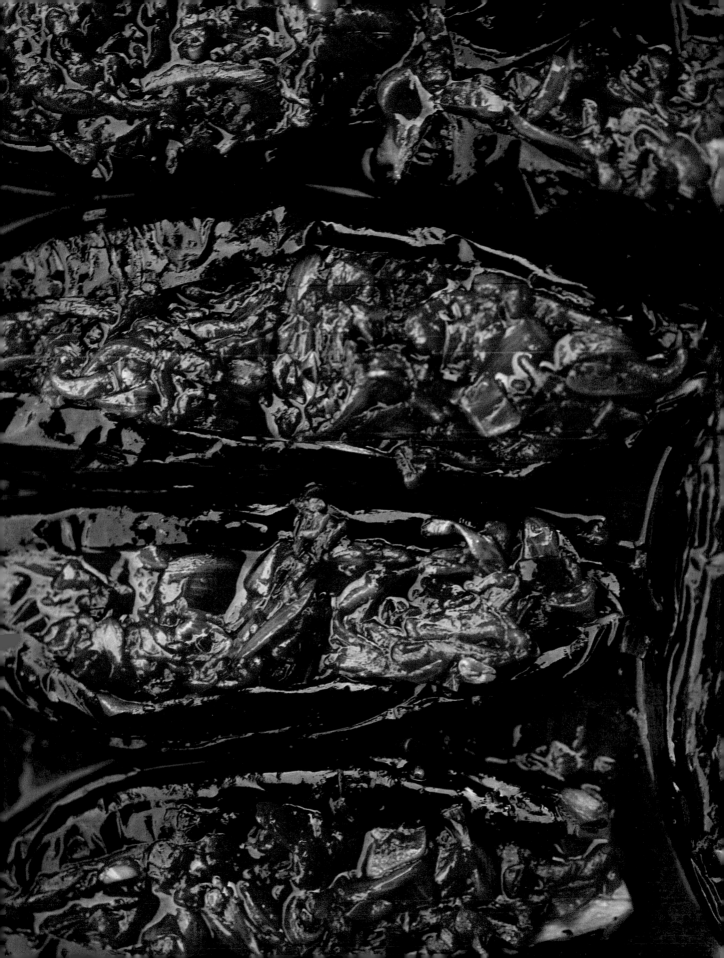

chicken soup with lemon and rice

κοτόσουπα αυγολέμονο

This dish needs a good many hungry mouths and should be eaten when the moon is on the wane. Everyone knows that guests tend to get a little too rowdy if you hold dinner parties when there is a full moon!

serves 6

1 x 2kg (4½lb) chicken, left whole
1 bouquet garni (parsley stems, celery leaves, and bay leaves tied into a bundle with string)
salt and pepper to taste
500g (18oz) carrots, left whole
500g (18oz) small potatoes, left whole
500g (18oz) leeks, white and soft green part, trimmed and rinsed
½ bunch flat-leaf parsley
125g (4½oz) short-grain rice
3 eggs, separated
75–100ml (2½–3½fl oz) lemon juice

to serve
olive oil
juice of 1 lemon

1   Put the chicken, bouquet garni, and some salt in a large pot. Cover with cold water, bring to the boil, and skim off any impurities that rise to the surface. Lower the heat and simmer. The chicken will be cooked in about 70 minutes.

2   When the chicken is cooked, use a straining spoon to transfer it to a large bowl. Add the carrots and potatoes to the liquid and cook until they're soft – about 15 minutes. Transfer to the bowl with the chicken.

3   Add the leeks and parsley to the liquid and blanch for 10 minutes. When the leeks are ready, put them and the parsley with the chicken.

4   Line a fine mesh sieve with dampened cheesecloth and set it over a large bowl. Ladle the liquid into the bowl through the cheesecloth. Do not use any of the impurities that remain at the bottom of the pot as they will turn your stock cloudy. Measure the stock: it should not exceed 1.5 litres (2¾ pints); if it does, return to the heat and reduce.

5   Return the stock to the pot, bring to simmering point, and add the rice. Simmer for 5–8 minutes.

6   Meanwhile, in a large bowl, whisk the egg whites to a soft peak, then add the yolks and whisk to blend. Add a ladleful of warm soup to the egg mixture and whisk to blend. Pour the mixture back in the soup pot, add 75ml (2½fl oz) of the lemon juice and whisk softly until well blended. Switch off the heat, leave the pot on the stove, and stir for 5 minutes. Taste for seasoning and sharpness. If you wish, add more lemon juice.

7   Pick the meat from the bones, slice the vegetables, and put it all on a platter. Dress with the olive oil and lemon juice, and serve with the soup.

salata horiatiki

σαλάτα χωριάτικη

This tomato, cucumber, green pepper, and feta salad is the ancestor of all those dubious Greek salads you find in restaurants everywhere. The real thing conjures up all the glories of September: the fields of ripe tomatoes, a suntanned face and dried, sun-etched lips, touched by the smell of the fruit and the warmth of the seasons.

serves 4

1kg (2⅓lb) knobbly tomatoes
1 cucumber, the smaller the better
100g (3½oz) pale green peppers
100g (3½oz) white onions
sea salt
500g (18oz) barrel-matured feta
  cheese
½ bunch flat-leaf parsley
a few large Greek olives
a few Santorinian caper leaves

dressing

150ml (5fl oz) extra virgin olive oil
  (mild oil from the early harvest
  is best for this salad)
3 tbsp aged Corinthian red wine
  vinegar
salt and pepper to taste

1   Cut the tomatoes into wedges. Peel the cucumber, halve lengthways, and cut into uneven, thickish pieces. Seed and thinly slice the peppers. Peel and thinly slice the onions, then scrub them with sea salt and rinse well under the cold-water tap – this makes them taste milder. Break the cheese into small pieces in your fingers. Finely chop the parsley.

2   Place all the salad ingredients, including the olives and caper leaves, together in a large bowl. An hour before serving, mix the dressing ingredients well in a small jar with a lid, pour over the salad, and toss. The longer you leave the salad with the dressing, the better the dressing will taste.

3   You'll need a very large loaf of good sourdough bread to go with this salad.

tirokafteri

τυροκαυτερή

This is a delicious coarse purée of cheese. As well as looking good among the mezedes, *it will go well with any cold meats.*

serves 6–8

400g (14oz) red onions

200g (7oz) feta cheese

100g (3½oz) Kefalotiri cheese (a
  hard sheep's milk cheese)

100g (3½oz) Metsovone cheese
  (a medium-hard smoked sheep's
  milk cheese)

100g (3½oz) pickled green
  chilli peppers, seeded, and
  finely diced

40g (1½oz) flat-leaf parsley,
  finely chopped

1 bunch thyme, leaves stripped
  and stalks discarded

200ml (7fl oz) extra virgin olive oil

salt and pepper to taste

1   Preheat the oven to 180°C/350°F/gas mark 4.

2   Roast the onions whole in their skins until the insides are so soft that you can squeeze the flesh out. Discard the skins and chop the red onion pulp.

3   Crumble the feta into a bowl with your fingers and break the other cheeses into small pieces. Add to the feta with all the other ingredients. Mix well. Check the seasoning.

seasonal green fritters

τηγανίτες με χορταρικά

These fresh green fritters are sensational when eaten hot. There are some dishes that inspire diners to hang around in the kitchen eating them as fast as they are made, and this is one of them!

serves 6–8

55g (2oz) each of small spinach leaves, rocket leaves, mustard leaves, and beetroot leaves
½ bunch dill
1 celery stick
1 bunch spring onions
½ fennel bulb
salt and pepper to taste
groundnut oil for frying
15g (½oz) butter

batter

250g (9oz) plain flour (type "00" pasta flour is good)
375ml (13fl oz) sparkling mineral water

1 Chop the spinach, rocket, mustard, beetroot, and dill leaves. Feel free to substitute other seasonal green leaves or leave out any that are unavailable. Trim and finely dice the celery and spring onions and add to the leaves. Use a vegetable peeler to cut the fennel into fine shavings. Add to the leaves.

2 Sprinkle the mixture with salt, leave for 10 minutes, then wash well, squeezing out as much water as possible. Mix everything together thoroughly.

3 Make the batter by whisking the flour and water together until smooth: you can keep it in the refrigerator, but it is better fresh. Using a spoon, add the greens to the batter at a ratio of two portions of batter to one of greens. You can make the fritters any size you fancy. Season well.

4 Heat the oil and butter together in a frying pan and drop in spoonfuls of the mixture. Cook on both sides until crisp. Eat hot with *tzatziki* (see page 165).

home-made filo

σπιτικό φύλλο

I know that you can buy filo in packets, but I beg you to try making it yourself at least once, as it is a much easier process than you would imagine. And if you are one of the growing band of cooks with a pasta machine, you really have no excuse not to make it at all!

makes about 1kg (2¼lb) pastry

300g (10½oz) "00" type white
   pasta flour
300g (10½oz) strong white bread
   flour
2 tbsp extra virgin olive oil
2 tsp white wine vinegar
275ml (9½fl oz) water, with a
   little extra if necessary
2 tsp salt

1   Mix all the ingredients together in a large bowl. This quantity is small enough to make by hand, but you could use a food processor.

2   When the dough has "come together", knead thoroughly. Filo takes about 10–15 minutes of kneading. When it is ready, the dough should have a very soft and silky feel to it.

3   Wrap the dough in clingfilm and keep it in the refrigerator overnight, or for as long as 4 days.

4   To turn filo dough into sheets, nothing beats a pasta machine. Run the dough through until you have made it as thin as possible. Dust the individual sheets with flour and keep under a damp cloth while you are working. You can make filo without a pasta machine, but you will need a lot of time, patience and a very long, thin rolling pin. The pastry is now ready for use.

basic avgolemono sauce

αυγολέμονο

The most basic Greek sauce of all!

makes about 700ml (1 ¼ pints)

2 eggs, separated
500ml (18fl oz) "light" stock
(chicken or pan juices,
depending on what you are
making)
juice of 2 lemons
salt and pepper to taste

1 Using a whisk, beat the egg whites until they form a stiff foam.

2 Slowly add a ladleful of the pan juices to the egg whites, whisking continuously.

3 Add the egg yolks.

4 Add another ladleful of the pan juices, then add the lemon juice and keep whisking for a couple more minutes.

5 Season with salt and pepper to taste.

"…ouzo drinking is an art, and maybe also a way of life. But it's not the ouzo that counts – it's who you drink it with. Ouzo tastes best when it is drunk at home and is a merry catalyst for good times, but the key to drinking ouzo is to eat mezedes with it."

thank you

With any project as long and complicated as a book there are many people both directly and indirectly involved in its creation. So Charles and I have a great many people to thank.

More than thanks are due to Panagiotis Manuelidis the man behind Odysea, but above all a friend and my Greek food mentor. Odysea is the only supplier of Greek products to the three Real Greek restaurants in London, and we are grateful for their support and advice.

Roussas for showing us the traditional way to produce authentic barrel-matured Greek feta, and for his delicious cheese.

The Greek Embassy in London for support, help and encouragement at every stage. Victoria Solomonidou, the Greek cultural attaché in London, for constant support of the Real Greek, for telling the story of Saint Fanourios, and for baking the cake that commemorates the name of the saint.

For the team in the kitchens of the Real Greek restaurants, particularly Alasdair Fraser, Danny Marshall, George Logothetis, and Luke Cleghorn, who shouldered the burden while I took time out to write the book and travel to Greece for the photography.

Miranda Harvey, the designer, for making the book look so good. And Jason Lowe for stunning photographs and for listening to all my ramblings about Greek food and culture. Both of them helped to produce a book quintessentially Greek in style.

Rebecca Spry for managing to cope with our Greek way of doing things; Susan Fleming for editing with a such a light touch; Jane Suthering for her advice and recipe testing; and Yasia Williams for organizing the trips to Greece.

Everyone who lives and works at the cooperative of Rovies. This is where we stayed to do the food photography, and they have always been my only supplier of fine Greek olives. Visiting the cooperative is like going to the home of an old friend who has never complained about the thirst or cold, and even in the midst of change has remained constant.

Particular thanks to "Thia" Argini for making us feel at home in her house, and for giving us the run of her kitchen. Also to Koula Georgiou, one of the best Greek cooks I have ever met, for helping with the cooking for the book's photography and for looking after us during our stay in Rovies. Marina and Stephanos Valli, the owners of the Eleonas apartments in Rovies, for their hospitality and for showing us the beautiful mountains of Evia. Also their daughter Argini, for her perceptive comments about the food, good company, and for helping us to set up the Greek Easter outdoor table. And Vangelis, one of the shepherds of the cooperative of Rovies, not only for introducing us to his herd, but for sacrificing an "Easter lamb".

Meanwhile in London, while we were working on the book, Paloma Campbell my business partner was at work on another project – Freddie, a beautiful child born in 2003! Despite the trials of pregnancy, Paloma found time to rule the restaurants and still make her inimitable comments on my written English!

But most of all I must dedicate this book to my parents, Tjeni and Ptolemaios. They gave me my respect for Greek food and cooking; they shared their recipes and gave me unfailing advice. Their love and courage inspires everything I do.

Theodore Kyriakou

index